Praise fo

The
FRESH START
PROMISE

"Edwige's spirit is contagious, and her great wisdom is a result of her personal struggle and wonderful success. If you want to lift up your mind, body, and spirit, read her book, *The Fresh Start Promise*."

—Barbara Corcoran,
founder of The Corcoran Group, New York City

"Edwige brings a warmth, honesty and practicality that few can match. She has been using techniques rooted in spirituality, self-actualization, meditation, hypnotherapy, and common sense for decades, long before it was trendy to do so. Edwige is a gifted individual able to ground these techniques into useful pathways for real change. Her practical advice seems to speak to each person ... to create avenues for them to make astonishing breakthroughs and actually change their lives for the better."

—Carol Scott,
founder and CEO, ECA World Fitness

"Finally, a book that clearly addresses the issues of energetic and emotional imbalance as significant obstacles to health and well-being. For those seeking joy that comes with lasting life improvement and change, *The Fresh Start Promise* is a must-read."

—Dr. Todd Sinett,
author of *The Truth About Back Pain*

"I have seen hundreds of clients whose joyous and healthy lives come from following Edwige's vision—her words, practices, and suggestions that you will carry with you and within you for all time."

—Marjorie Jaffe,
author of *The Muscle Memory Method*

"Edwige has a unique ability to motivate individuals to pursue and attain their goals. Her bright and optimistic spirit, along with her warmth and humility, will allow her readers to believe in the promise of a healthier, more fulfilling and vibrant lifestyle."

—Mary Bohnen,
Director of Client Services, Freedom Institute

The
FRESH START
PROMISE

28 Days to Total Mind, Body, Spirit
Transformation

Edwige Gilbert

Llewellyn Publications
Woodbury, Minnesota

First Edition
First Printing, 2008

Book design by Joanna Willis
Cover art courtesy of the author
Cover design by Ellen Dahl

Llewellyn is a registered trademark of Llewellyn Worldwide, Ltd.

Library of Congress Cataloging-in-Publication Data
Gilbert, Edwige.
 The fresh start promise : 28 days to total mind, body, spirit transformation / Edwige Gilbert.—1st ed.
  p.   cm.
Includes index.
ISBN 978-0-7387-1322-9
1. Change (Psychology) 2. Self-help techniques. I. Title.
BF637.C4G54 2007
646.7—dc22

                                                                2007044436

Llewellyn Publications
A Division of Llewellyn Worldwide, Ltd.
2143 Wooddale Drive, Dept. 978-0-7387-1322-9
Woodbury, MN 55125-2989, U.S.A.
www.llewellyn.com

Printed in the United States of America

To my grandmother for her life lessons
To my mother for her spirit of *joie de vivre*

Contents

WEEK THREE: THE SPIRIT
I WILL

WEEK FOUR: DECLARING VICTORY

Index of Practices and Meditations

MIND-BASED MEDITATIONS

To release burdens of worry, stress, and anxiety, this inspiring meditation supports change and offers sustenance on challenging days.

Especially when done together with the Sword of Fearlessness (below), this meditation manifests warrior conviction, purpose, and invincibility.

To manifest strength and courage, use this meditation anytime, preparing first with the 3Cs.

This meditation helps manifest desired outcomes, desired futures—and the inspiration and perseverance needed for the journey.

BODY-BASED PRACTICES

Use the Chi Ball Practice to discover, and rediscover, this primary life energy. The Chi Belly Massage and Chi Body Massage are to be practiced every day to maintain vibrant energy.

This head-to-toe breathing practice is for emotional balancing.

Evening Cleansing Rituals

Wrist Shake . . . 94

Arm Swing . . . 102

Spinal Cord Breathing . . . 116

These rituals release stressful or sluggish energy and restore balance to the body; they can be combined with Energizing Rituals as needed.

Sound Therapy: An Introduction . . . 94

These six healing sounds release intense emotions such as anger, fear, and sadness; they can be practiced together for emotional balancing or used separately as the need arises.

Finger Therapy: An Introduction . . . 95

These "finger-grabbing" exercises, one for each finger, are used to clear negative emotions. (To combine all five, see page 140.)

Breath Therapy for Emotional Balancing . . . 99

These three techniques restore equilibrium when one is angry, in need of nurture, or feeling disoriented.

Five Bites Technique for Mindful Eating . . . 112

This mealtime practice helps create a new healthy conditioning regarding eating habits and also promotes weight loss.

Mindful Warrior Walk . . . 123

This practice restores yin-yang balance; connects the feet to the energy of the earth and the head to the energy of the sky, and creates a mindful experience of the present moment; it can be used anytime.

Emergency Release Therapy . . . 140

This therapy is for use at times of high stress and emotion; it helps clear upset, anger, sadness, depression.

Sound and Finger Therapy Combined ... 145

Combining the healing sounds and the finger-grab technique, this practice is for mind/body rebalancing.

BODY-BASED MEDITATIONS

Starlit Sky ... 127

This sleep-inducing practice works wonders for insomnia.

The Lighthouse ... 137

This practice is for use when feeling sick or under the weather; it can be used at any time to help dispel aches and pains.

SPIRIT-BASED PRACTICES

The Optimizing Faculties of Joie de Vivre

These techniques help cultivate six qualities essential to a joyful life.

SPIRIT-BASED MEDITATIONS

The Diamond in the Heart ... 191

To establish a loving connection to the self, this practice can be used anytime.

The Garden of the Heart ... 199

This practice, too, is for cultivating loving kindness to the self and can be used anytime.

The Golden Chalice . . . 207

To cultivate abundance, practice this meditation.

The Satellite . . . 213

This meditation helps to reconcile with others and reestablish loving connections.

The Night Walk . . . 228

To develop awareness of intuition, this peaceful meditation has great power.

Acknowledgments

I was lucky to have two literary agents on this journey: first and foremost, I would like to thank Denise Marcil, who believed in me and my work and who had the foresight and vision to see that Fresh Start (the program) could become *The Fresh Start Promise* (the book), and who was my first guide on my journey into publishing. I would also like to thank my second agent, Jennie Dunham, who worked so diligently to bring this project home. To Carrie Obry, at Llewellyn, who believed in this project and proved it by working so patiently with me to bring it to press. To Nellie Sabin, who laid the groundwork for *Fresh Start* and pointed me in the right direction. To Mark Kusnir, for hearing my voice and helping me translate it onto the written page, and for bringing the language of joy, humor, spirit, and magic to *The Fresh Start Promise*.

To Marjorie Jaffe, a leader in Mind-Body Integration who taught me so much about that field; to Carol Scott, founder of East Coast Alliance, for the opportunity to develop my voice in the fitness world; to Dr. Sheldon and Todd Sinnett for clarifying for me the relationship between emotions and the body. To Dr. Evelyn Rappoport, a wise advisor in the field of psychotherapy; to Dr. Francis Clifton, who taught me the power of storytelling. To Kevin Barry Heany, director of the Addiction Institute of New York, who allowed me to develop the Fresh Start program. To Marie Bohnen, director of the Freedom Institute, who helped me implement the Fresh Start program.

To Janet Lowry, Meredith Cohen, and Marlene Oser, first friends who made me feel welcome in this country. To Veena Merchant, who believed in me; to Ilene Pacun, who shared my vision. To Rona Levine, who gave me wise counsel—as a writer and as a friend. To Louise Sarabella for finding Mark, for Marian Velez for her support, to Tinal Penzal for her love. To Shelly Sherri for her guidance, to Marie-Therese Ancellin and Lawrence Rosenthal for their French inspiration. To Audrey Heckler, for her encouragement; to Patricia Gorton, Michel Lalou, and Giamparo Paoletti for their marketing advice; to Susan Krausz, Marida Sapichino, and Heather Henderson for their great spirit.

Most of all, I would like to thank Allison Gilbert, my stepdaughter, for caring, my stepsister Karen Alter-Reed for always being there, and my stepbrothers Stuart and Kenny for supporting me in my vision. To my brother and sister-in-law Peter and Caroline Bade for their encouragement, to my stepfather, Jerome Alter, for his unconditional love and support, and of course to my mother, for life and love. To Sophie, my Maltese dog, for her faithful companionship. Finally, I would like to especially thank my husband John, for allowing me the time, for giving me encouragement, support, and his great love.

Introduction

> ## Attention! S'il vous plait!
>
> This book can cause profound alterations in attitude, including but not limited to: boundless energy, enthusiasm, purposefulness, and the French *joie de vivre*. Persons who wish to remain anxious, depressed, and immobilized are warned *not* to read this book due to the risk of positive life changes.

I think you picked up this book because you know, in your heart of hearts, that your life could be different—completely, wonderfully, astoundingly different! And that, quite simply, is the promise of this book and its twenty-eight-day program: from where you are now, you can move to the life you've always known would be yours, the life you've always imagined.

The Fresh Start Promise is, above all, a book of changes—complete life changes. It's about transforming the actual day-to-day conditions of your life to finally arrive at those life changes you've always been seeking. This program is about working with the mind to dissolve the obstacles that prevent change; it's about engaging the mind's creative power to define the life changes you seek. It's also about changing your relationship with your body: how you see it, how you treat it, how it treats you!

You will achieve optimal levels of vibrant physical energy, you will arrive at energetic and emotional balance, and you will transform your relationship with food. Finally, the program is about re-awakening your connection to the spirit to achieve profoundly deeper levels of honesty, compassion, and joy. It's about engaging the spirit to connect to yourself and others and, in the process, becoming a fully integrated human being, experiencing laughter, love, and *joie de vivre!* Because ultimately, *The Fresh Start Promise* is about joy . . . the French-inspired joy of life that I refused to abandon when I left my native France, a joy you will encounter in full detail when you reconnect to your spirit in the third and final stage of your journey.

Does this all sound too good to be true? I can only say that you can't possibly know until you try. Life change comes only with practice! If you choose to turn your back on this opportunity for personal transformation, that's up to you, of course, but I don't think you will. After all, we are talking about twenty-eight days that will change your world. Are you willing to give it a try, to take the chance, to take this opportunity for total mind, body, and spirit transformation? Come with me on this journey now, my dear reader! You have, after all, absolutely nothing to lose and everything to gain—I mean everything!

Please allow me to briefly describe how I came to offer others this powerful program. You see, *The Fresh Start Promise* has its roots in my own pursuit of meaningful life change. For more than thirty years now, I have been undertaking an exhaustive study of a wide variety of religions, disciplines, philosophies, and mind-body regimens. On this journey, I have been fortunate to study with leaders in psychology, spirituality, and mind-body awareness. During my study, I earned certifications as a yoga and Chi Gong instructor, fitness and aerobics instructor, hypnotherapist, substance abuse counselor, and neurolinguistic coach. Along the way, I learned to reconcile many diverse approaches to human wellness by looking for common threads and universal truths. Over time, I have taken the essential elements of everything I have learned and combined them in a new way, creating a powerful synergy among traditions from all over the world. Most importantly, I have been successfully using these techniques with my many clients. They work—this I can tell you! *The Fresh Start Promise* is, then, the ultimate wellness cookbook, combining tried and tested recipes from all the places I have lived and studied.

This book simplifies for you all the universal concepts of a joyful life. My clients love this program because it gives them the bottom-line results they seek without years of reading and classes. I have used this program successfully with hundreds of people suffering from a wide variety of conditions, from obesity to anxiety to phobias to addiction recovery; I have used it with children who have attention deficit disorders—and most importantly, I have used it on myself.

You see, my passage into this life was difficult. As I struggled to be born, my mother had an emergency cesarean. She was not expected to live, but somehow she summoned the energy to survive the trauma. My birth left me so oxygen deprived that I was not expected to live either, but luckily I shared my mother's genes. Somehow between my instinct for survival and the skills of a dedicated nurse, I lived to tell this tale.

Not long after this, as a little girl in France, I was placed in my grandmother's care while my parents went to America to seek their fortune. Perhaps because of my precarious entry into this world, my grandmother saw me as a fragile, helpless child who needed protection. She constantly tried to spare me from pain or failure by saying, "You can't do that." Burdened by this overprotective love, I became, you guessed it, a creature both fearful and shy—a walking invitation for a rescue mission. With everything done for me by others, I was without an ounce of confidence in my own abilities.

When I was nine, a schoolteacher called me to the blackboard to recite a poem. I will never forget that moment. There I stood in front of the class, my feet glued to the floor, heart jumping out of my chest, head pounding. I was convinced I would faint. Above it all, I heard the teacher's voice calling my name for all to hear, "Edwige, naughty little girl. You didn't study the poem, did you? Go back to your seat, Edwige." I walked back to my desk filled with relief and shame.

Fifteen years later, nothing had changed—in fact, I was even worse off! I was living in New York now, but I was profoundly uneasy with myself. Within months of my arrival upon these shores, my life was falling apart. Within a year, it had completely unraveled. Things were not going well in the new world! I was listless, unmotivated, without direction. Lady Liberty's words certainly applied to me: *tired . . . poor . . .* emotionally *wretched . . .* spiritually *homeless . . .* my life was *tempest-tossed.* I was, in short, a *huddled mess!*

The first major distress was my body: my weight was ballooning appallingly. You see, I had switched from a Mediterranean diet to a bagel-brownie diet instead. Gone was the svelte, chic young Frenchwoman. I was now twenty-five pounds overweight, an oversized immigrant. Next, my mind was in distress: it was anxious, fearful, melancholic. I was an absolute human shipwreck. Relationships? A hit from the disco era summed it up perfectly: *Once upon a time I was falling in love, now I'm only falling apart.*[1]

On some nights, alone in my apartment, I stood in front of a mirror sobbing inconsolably. What had become of my *self*? Where was Edwige? I could not say, I simply did not know. I knew only that I was a walking disaster, a French-American mess. A monumental mess—formidable, in the negative sense of the word! I had lost myself, and worse, I had lost my most precious gift, my *joie de vivre.*

In leaving France and my grandmother, I had left the only structure I had ever known, you see. Though the overprotective support of a parent or grandparent is not an ideal foundation for adult life, it is, at least, a framework. In America, I was formless, with no psychological infrastructure whatsoever. In France I was bound, but in America I dangled.

One day, at my wit's end and feeling powerless to stop or even slow the decline of "Edwige in America," I took some advice—my father's, actually. At his suggestion, I applied to become a guide at the United Nations. He believed this would be the sure cure for my shyness and, thanks to one of his friends, I was selected. *Mon dieu,* was I terrified!

---

1 From "Total Eclipse of the Heart," © 1982 by Jim Steinman.

After a month of tortuous training, my turn came to present the tour to sixty other trainees. The spotlight was on me. Can you guess what happened? Panic-stricken, I stood in the same place I had occupied fifteen years earlier in that cold French classroom.

The tour I gave was a disaster. Terrified, mumbling, babbling, I led my peers and our teacher through the chambers of the General Assembly and the Security Council. We had just visited the Japanese Peace Bell when another voice rang out. The voice was calm and clear, but still deeply upsetting. Once again, a teacher was cutting my miserable performance short. The practice tour aborted, the teacher asked me to see her at the administrative office that afternoon.

Later, as I walked down that endless corridor, my head filled with shameful thoughts. *What will my father say when I try to explain why I was fired before I even began? Grandmother was right, I'm a hopeless case. I can't do anything right! This is surely the bottom . . .*

Somehow I mustered the courage to enter the office, where the teacher waited for me. At her invitation, I sat down. I dropped my head and stared at the floor, ready for the guillotine. Silence filled the room.

"Edwige, look at me." Ever obedient, I raised my head to see a model of confidence and elegance addressing me. "Edwige, you remind me of myself, you know." *What?* I was dumbfounded. *What was she saying?*

Then it camwe to me. My body flooded with relief; the acid burn of anxiety vanished. Here was a true teacher! Here, for perhaps for the first time in my life, was the voice of compassion and understanding. "Edwige, listen carefully. Though today you can't possibly know it, like me, you will overcome your shyness. And in time, you will be one of the best UN guides I have ever trained."

What did this woman see in me? How did she know the very thing I needed the most? Belief. Affirmation. Faith. Within the year I had been selected the best new UN tour guide. I was interviewed on the radio, held up as a model for other young guides. This woman, my first true teacher, had believed in me when I could not believe in myself.

This was the first step of my own journey to a Fresh Start. It all began with belief—not my own, but that of another caring person. In time I would find my own belief, my own voice, my own insights. There were countless obstacles and mistakes along the way, of course. Armed only with another's message of belief, and without any real knowledge of myself, I took wrong turns. I got lost so often that it seemed every other turn was a wrong turn.

My first goal was my body. Overweight? Okay, well, the problem must be food. I tried a total of twenty-three diets, and all of them failed. Finally I settled on the simplest solution possible: starvation. Overweight means too many calories, right? Well, stop eating, then! And that's what I did. I starved myself thin. Sure, I was a little pale. True, I barely had the energy to climb a short flight of stairs, and any conversation longer than three minutes exhausted me mentally. Okay, I had constant headaches, a perpetual ringing in my ears. So what? I was thin, *d'accord*? I was thin!

On a roll now, I began to exercise. Starvation wasn't enough, you see. And no, not just a little jogging and light weight training. My physical regimen was Olympian; there simply weren't enough hours in the day for it. Luckily some kind soul at the gym suggested that with exercise morning, noon, and night, I might consider increasing my food intake just a little. Without that advice, I would have hit bottom that much sooner.

And so it went. If there was a journey to be made, I was all for it. My own journey, however, was to the extremes, to ever greater imbalance. Here, in America, anything was possible! I could adopt as many extreme approaches as I wanted to. That became my specialty: I was so adept I could juggle several extremes at once. Eventually I threw yoga into my ever-expanding regimen. This was a blessing, it turned out, for with yoga came my first connection to the wisdom of the East and an entirely new concept . . . balance! But even then, I completely missed the boat at first. What a great idea! Balance! Of course! How could I have missed it? Here was my new goal, and I was aggressive in its pursuit. Each day, from dawn to dusk, I relentlessly sought balance. I would accept nothing less! Over time, after many courses and much study, I finally arrived at the actual meaning of the word—lucky, perhaps, for if I hadn't, my search for balance would likely have destroyed me.

Perhaps I am rendering it comically here, but this story is true, dear reader. In my first months in "the land of the free," my life was indeed free: free of structure and coherence. The structure I had grown up with in France was oppressive, but it had at least supported me. When I lost this, I lost myself. Yet without the physical, mental, and emotional chaos that followed after my move to America, I would still be lost. And you wouldn't be reading these words, I can assure you. My journey to health and wellness began only when I saw its necessity. It may take time, but the drops of wisdom that one gains from guides along the path, from study and consideration . . . they do finally penetrate the consciousness. Insights begin to accrue.

One day, leaving one of my countless fitness classes, I overheard a startling conversation in the elevator. Two women, clearly friends, were talking of some difficulty, some life challenge or other, and I listened idly. When one of them spoke the phrase "safe place," the words stuck instantly in my consciousness. I stood immobilized as the elevator reached the lobby and the women exited, glancing quizzically back at me. The doors closed and the elevator ascended again, my thoughts with it. *What?* I wondered to myself. *There exists a safe place, a place for people in times of emotional distress?* I was enthralled. I was appalled. *Where is this place? How do you get there? Who has the key? Why hasn't anyone told me about this place?!* Apparently Grandmother hadn't known of it herself. Poor Grandmother, and poor Edwige!

This "chance revelation"—don't believe it, nothing is by chance!—changed my life completely. In my pursuit of happiness in America I had become utterly unhappy. Upon my arrival, what little there was of me crumbled completely. When I embarked upon a journey of change, at first I changed myself for the worse. The harder I tried, the worse things became. Then came this key, the one I hold out to you now.

The key of all successful life change is emotional safety. Above all else in this world we need a place of sanctuary from life's tribulations, from its inevitable negative emotions. Fear, anger, anxiety, sadness—the four horsemen of the emotional apocalypse—these can sabotage our efforts at change. But such emotions are not themselves the problem.

They cannot be avoided. They are a part of life, and to hope to escape them is a fantasy, an illusion. The problem is that we are missing that safe place within, the place beyond the reach of the horsemen. Without a healthy internal structure, we become paralyzed by the horsemen, by the negative emotions that can trample our hope for lasting life change. The overeating, the excessive drinking, the compulsive exercising, the obsessions . . . these are not the problem. They are merely a deliberate attempt—often a desperate one—to insulate the fragile self from the sting of these negative emotions.

Rising in the elevator that day, all this became clear to me. Don't attack the symptoms. Don't try to fight off the horsemen, Edwige. Wrong, wrong, wrong. No, the opposite is necessary. Find safety, find a refuge. Take refuge in the self, the deeper, calmer, compassionate self. Once there, once safe, once strong, then you can work from the inside out. *Clear* the negative emotions, *create* the vision required for change. Return to the safe place whenever necessary; know that it always waits for you.

Armed with this overheard epiphany, I was unstoppable. On that day, in an Otis elevator, the Fresh Start program was conceived. This book's origins are in that moment. I still had much to learn, of course—*how* to clear, *how* to create, for example—but finally I could see the substance beneath my feet; finally the path had emerged.

Here, finally, was the formula . . . here was the foundation for change.

. . . .

I hold out this formula to you now, dear reader. I offer you this foundation for change. Will you join me on this platform? Here is the voice for change, lasting life change. Do you hear it? Do you accept it? Do you believe in its power to forever transform you?

. . . .

Since my inauspicious beginnings, I have fully transformed my life. Today I have my own business, New Life Directions. I am happily married. I am confident, clear about my purpose, clear about where I'm going. I love who I am! Getting from there to here was quite a journey, and along the way I have faced new fears, developed greater strengths, reevaluated my most important relationships, and created a vision of what I wanted to be and to accomplish. This book is, then, the accumulated wisdom and knowledge of my journey to change—a compilation of the best practices I found first for myself, because it was I who needed them most. My transformation took me through disappointment, pain, failure, and loss—all the things my grandmother had warned me about. But much more significantly, it brought clarity, purpose, love, and joy into my life. Like everyone else, I still have moments of doubt and weakness. The difference is that today I know who I am: a strong, successful, self-sufficient human being, one who copes actively, not passively. My grandmother would be proud!

Remember When Anything Seemed Possible?

Little children think they can do anything. They try to fly, or hatch dinosaurs, or make magic potions out of chocolate milk. Why not? For children everything is possible.

Maybe you can remember a time when you believed the world was full of mystery and possibility, a time when your plans for the afternoon included being queen or king of your own castle, a time when you knew you'd grow up to be famous or do something fantastic. You took it for granted that anything was possible. You simply believed!

And as you grew up, perhaps other people showed confidence in you. Successful adults often credit a parent or a guardian's absolute belief in their abilities as the source of their later success.

Barbara Corcoran, who built the Corcoran real estate empire in New York from scratch, recalls her childhood in her book *Use What You've Got.* Her mother always told her, "Barbara, you can do anything you want." So she did! It helps to have supportive parents telling you from birth that you are capable of anything, doesn't it?

Oprah Winfrey was a child born into very difficult circumstances. She credits both her grandmother and her father for providing her the love, discipline, and support that were required to turn her life around. Paul Newman cites his mother's support and belief for his early success as an actor. The list goes on: many people in the public eye have early believers to thank.

These are the lucky ones, of course. Some people have achieved their success without any parental support whatsoever, relying almost solely on their own capacity for self-belief. Arnold Schwarzenegger, as a notable example, believes his success, first as world champion bodybuilder, then as an actor, and now as governor of California, grew out of his capacity for engaging in positive self-belief and for using the power of imagination to create his desired outcomes.

To produce change in our lives, we need the power of belief and imagination: a power that children have but many adults lose. We are not talking here about self-delusion. We mean to rediscover our ability to imagine what we would really like to be, to rediscover our voice of self-belief, to learn to use mental reconditioning to bring us power and move us toward our goals and dreams. So come with me now and rediscover your power of belief!

· · · · · · · · · · · · · · · ·

Every day, millions of people wake up thinking, "Today I am going to do things differently!" Every spring, millions start thinking about summer clothes and getting into shape. Every New Year's eve, millions make resolutions. Everybody has the impulse for a new beginning.

When trying to bring about change in their lives, however, most people reach for the only tool they think they have: willpower. They think it's possible to *force* change upon themselves through acts of will. Most often, unfortunately, not only do they fall short of the finish line, they actually lose ground.

American culture values problem-solving ability, and willpower is considered one of the greatest virtues. We have inherited the belief that frontiers are to be conquered, and hard work is rewarded. We believe that problems have to be solved no matter the cost. Thus we have abundant information about how to solve just about anything. But alas, human beings are complex creatures who cannot be treated with standardized solutions and formulas. In our approaches to personal change we have invested too heavily in intellectual knowledge and not enough in the wisdom of common sense—and practice. With shelves of self-help books offering a bewildering array of contradictory methods of change, we are overdosing on knowledge-based solutions. Just look at dieting. Americans spend $109 million on dieting and diet products every day, according to the U.S. Department of Health and Human Services. Nearly two-thirds are overweight: 25 percent of American men and 45 percent of American women are now dieting—but sadly, only 5 percent will meet their weight-loss goals and then maintain them.

How Can We Arrive at Lasting Change?

Change begins to be possible only when we understand that it is futile to struggle willfully against our habitual patterns of behavior. Instead we must shift our focus. As we rebalance our emotions, use the power of compelling images, and engage in kind words and inspiring thoughts, our minds will let us create new, healthier behaviors. The key to change is in moving away from pain and toward pleasure.

Take weight loss, for example. If you want to lose weight, the worst thing you can do is become obsessed with those extra pounds. That's too painful, too negative—it simply reinforces deeply entrenched negative attitudes. Successful life change requires something quite different. To lose that weight you need to engage your power of belief—you need to recondition your mental habits—you need to visualize how you would like to look and feel as a slim person. It's the vision that creates the change! This book will teach you how to envision.

This is where I come in, dear reader. I can help you create your new life; I can help you envision a new future! This is what I do—what I have been doing for over twenty years. This is how I've helped thousands of people fundamentally reimagine and redesign their lives. In twenty-eight days I will provide you with the new tools, the new vision, and the new language you need to successfully change your life. Come with me now and begin your journey!

What to Pack for This Journey

You'll want to travel light! In your backpack, include:

- an open mind
- an open heart
- belief in your strengths
- a sense of adventure
- the desire to pursue your truth
- a deep commitment to change

Leave room for things you will acquire along the way, including food for thought, centering techniques, and self-empowering declarations that will open your heart and make room for love, trust, and vibrant energy.

What You Need to Get Started

What do you need to start? Just an open mind and the willingness to commit to something new. You do not need special clothes, exotic foods, scented candles, healing crystals, an Indian guru, or a support group. Everything you need is in this book.

So I hope you are now committed! You want to change the conditions of your life, don't you? Now is the perfect time to prove you're serious. Go find a pen. (It's okay, I'll wait!) Now get ready to sign on the dotted line. Don't worry—this is between you and yourself. The Victory Contract is your promise to yourself, your commitment to your successful future.

I know some of you will be tempted to skip this contract. You might read it, consider it, but then not actually sign it. This may seem like a small omission, especially since nobody else will care if you sign it or not. But failing to sign your Victory Contract might mean you aren't really committed to this program.

What is stopping you? What would happen to your life if you surrendered to this book? It's a good question, is it not! If you are doubtful, consider this: by committing to this program, you are committing to yourself, affirming to your self that you deserve the life you've always dreamed of. Sure, at this point this only seems like a possibility, you're thinking. But let me put it to you this way: is this an opportunity you can afford to miss?

A client of mine starting the Fresh Start program read the Victory Contract and began to cry. She had never taken time for herself in her life, of course, and faced with making a commitment to her own happiness, she suddenly understood that she was about to embrace the most fundamental human right: the right to a fulfilling and rewarding life. Women so often feel the pressure of taking care of others. Men often feel the pressure of supporting others. Ironically, both do a much better job when they look after themselves first!

FRESH START
VICTORY CONTRACT

I, _____, recognize that:

- » I am a unique individual with a special purpose.
- » I am meant to have a rich and fulfilling life.
- » I am worthy of respect and self-respect.
- » I have within myself gifts, talents, strengths, and unrealized potential.
- » I create unconditional love and acceptance for myself.
- » I can choose a kind and caring attitude toward others.
- » I am capable of making my dreams a reality.

Therefore, I will:

- » be clear about my purpose.
- » be kind and loving toward myself and others.
- » look within for spiritual intelligence and guidance.
- » look at every challenge as an opportunity to further my dream.
- » discard outdated, counterproductive, and anxiety-producing ways of thinking.
- » see myself victorious.
- » rely on myself, not others, to transform my life from the inside out.
- » be open-minded and adventurous.

I will pursue my goals with clear intention and honesty. I am willing to do the work required to transform my attitude and my life. Nothing and no one can stop me from manifesting my vision of the person I desire to be.

_____   _____
Signature   Date

Congratulations! You did it! Now give yourself a hug and get ready for life change!

How You Will Use This Book

The Fresh Start Promise will lead you through a four-week program. In Weeks One, Two, and Three, we will address mind, body, and spirit. Each of these sections has two chapters that you will read that week:

- Each *concept chapter* explains that week's practice. It begins with an analysis of its topic (mind, body, spirit), then offers an inspiring exploration of the week's approaches to change.

- Each *practice chapter* offers day-by-day, step-by-step techniques and exercises. You will practice these for twenty minutes each morning and each evening, and during the day as called for.

The foundation of the Fresh Start Program can be summed up in three basic statements: *I can, I do, I will.* Each morning after you wake up, you will determine what you want to accomplish that day, then activate your daily plan with three core assertions: *I can, I do, I will.* Whenever you encounter difficult situations in your life, you will again assert, *I can, I do, I will.* And these are much more than simple affirmations, dear reader. The statement *I can* acts to free the mind and give permission for change. The statement *I do* ensures action to create the desired change. The statement *I will* mobilizes the spirit. Together they integrate the three levels of being—mind, body, and spirit—and create the power of intentional harmony: the essential secret to successful life change!

WEEK ONE
THE MIND

I Can

I Can

I Can

i can

I CAN

I CAN

I Can

I CAN

Whether you believe you can
or you believe you can't
you are right.
HENRY FORD

A man who is of "sound mind" is one
who keeps the inner madman
under lock and key.
PAUL VALÈRY

There is nothing so disobedient as an undisciplined mind.
There is nothing so obedient as a disciplined mind.
BUDDHA

We are what we repeatedly do.
ARISTOTLE

The mind is like a clock that is
constantly running down and must be
wound up daily with good thoughts.
FULTON J. SHEEN

You must do the thing that
you think you cannot do.
ELEANOR ROOSEVELT

1

Changing How You Think About Change

Welcome to chapter 1 and the first week of your Fresh Start. This is an exciting week—the week things finally begin to change! Over the next seven days, you will lay down a new life foundation by engaging in the process vital to life change: mental reconditioning. Let us begin this journey by considering the singular importance of the mind in all human lives, all accomplishments, all endeavors. Let us recognize the power of the mind and its ability to create life change. Let us give thought to *thought*.

Have you ever considered the truth of the idea that "we are what we think"? Henry Ford certainly knew this to be true. Like many others before and after him, he recognized that human thought is the alpha and omega of human experience. Think about it: what have you ever achieved that did not begin as a thought, a conception of the mind, an idea? Though we take it for granted, just as we take breathing for granted, thought determines the conditions of our everyday existence. It defines and establishes what we do and don't do today, what we will and won't do tomorrow, how we live and don't live. Thought, therefore, determines the quality of our lives. It can limit or liberate, imprison or set free, be a dead-end alley or an endless western frontier. What our thoughts are, and how they operate in our lives, is up to us! Our minds shape our lives. Acknowledging this truth can of itself change lives, for there is no greater earthly power than that of the human mind. Human thought determines human emotions, human emotions influence and determine decision-making and action, actions determine life outcomes. It all begins in thought—thought is destiny!

René Descartes said, "I think, therefore I am." That was a nice start, René, but the significance of human thought extends well beyond simply being. To fully grasp the importance of the mind in our lives, we need to reach deeper. We need to reach further back, to the wisdom of the East, to the enlightened thought of the Buddha, who told us that to assert control over the quality of our lives we need first to assert control over the quality of our thoughts.

Let me ask you now, dear reader, what is the quality of your thought? Do you feel you are in control of your mind? Do you feel that it does your will, that it helps you on your way, that it is a tool, an aid, that it is of constructive service in your life? Or, on the contrary, do you find yourself a victim of your thoughts? Do you find yourself battered and bruised by mental tendencies that are negative, limiting, hurtful? Are you the master or the slave? Do you possess your mind, or does it possess you? You think, therefore you are—but what, exactly, are you?

It has been said that a mind is a terrible thing to waste. This is true, unquestionably. But for our purposes here, let me put forward a variation on this theme. In its untrained, poorly behaved, destructive configuration, a mind is, more profoundly and more simply, a terrible thing! Those of my clients who are in rehab recovering from addiction know this all too well. There is nothing quite so daunting, limiting, and destructive as a fully distracted human mind.

How then do we move our minds beyond distraction? How then can we regain at least some degree of control over our thoughts—and thereby over our lives?

In India, the traditional metaphor for the unmanaged and unmanageable human mind is that of the "drunken monkey," with its constant, erratic movement up and down, to and fro, here and there. Since there aren't many monkeys where I live, I've always felt the need for a more appropriate metaphor. Sixteen years ago, Sophie the Maltese entered my life, and a new metaphor was born.

Ever since moving to America, I'd wanted a dog. I had grown up with dogs, you see. Poodles and chihuahuas, all perfectly behaved, all perfectly trained by—you guessed it—my dear grandmother. But in America I was my own master! I did my own research, consulted my own experts, and determined that the gentle and obedient Maltese would be the dog for me.

I arrived home with Sophie, the most adorable Maltese puppy imaginable, or so I thought. The truth was that Sophie was a terror; Sophie was an *enfant terrible.* This lovely little white ball of fur ran around the apartment, circling the sofa at such speed that she was a white blur. She jumped at me out of nowhere, nipped my legs and arms, and worst of all, bit my nose! Her teeth were tiny, but, *mon dieu,* were they sharp! Sophie was mad. I was madder!

I had imagined an adorable lap dog, but what I got was a raging little devil. In desperation, I sought the advice of a dog therapist. (Yes, in New York City even dogs have therapists.) The man's advice was simple: a dog without a master is a dog from hell. He told me I must assert mastery over Sophie. I must use intention, voice, and action to let her know who was in charge.

By month's end, Sophie was everything I had wanted: sweet, loving, cuddly. I was happy, she was happy. We've both been supremely contented ever since.

So I put this forward to you now, dear reader. If your mind is too often a terror, too often behaves like an untrained, uncontrollable puppy, a change of mind is in order for you. For your life to change, a change of mind must precede it.

Week One is the week the puppy gets trained! This is the week you begin to recondition your mind and become the master of your life.

. . . .

In the pursuit of meaningful life change, the trained mind becomes the greatest of all allies! The Fresh Start program begins with this process of mental training: we *clear and create*—clear the negative, create the positive.

Focused on negatives in the present, how can we achieve the positive outcomes we desire in our future? Before we can achieve anything constructive, we must first clear the mind's internal space, freeing it of its anxieties and stresses and agitations to give it the room and the light it needs to change. Take away the clouds and what do you have? Blue skies and radiant sunshine. This is the climate required by a healthy mind!

So here it is. The first step in creating desired changes in your life is to clear the present mind of its limiting, unproductive emotions. This is where your work begins, dear reader! Examine the contents of your mind right now. What are you feeling? What are you stressing over today? You know what I'm talking about. What's weighing on your mind? Now imagine clearing away all such negatively burdened thoughts. Imagine that they no longer pervade your thinking, your every mood. Imagine now the quiet, cloudless, sun-drenched place that lies within. Here is a place of comfort and safety and pleasure. Here is a place where all change becomes possible. This place exists, believe me! If you don't, think for a moment about the bright, sunlit faces of young saffron-robed Tibetan monks. Do you think their minds are cloudy?

All very nice, you say, *non*? Easier said than done, this clearing of the mind. Maybe fifteen or twenty years in an isolated monastery would do it. If this is your thinking, consider this: maybe that in itself is the problem. It is just such thoughts that sabotage change.

The technique you will learn in the next chapter will help you clear your mind by wiping away the dirt from the mirror of consciousness. I call it the 3Cs, and it is a foundational Fresh Start practice. Get ready to clear! Get ready to become *calm, centered*, and *connected*.

THE 3CS MEDITATION: THE PRACTICE OF CLEARING

Calm. Centered. Connected. The 3Cs meditation is the fundamental practice for clearing the mind. As medical research has demonstrated, meditation boosts positive emotions while simultaneously decreasing negative agitations. One name for its power to produce positive emotions, and thereby to produce positive life change, is neurogenesis. The field of neuroscience has shown that the architecture of the brain is not fixed but fluid, that permanent behavioral change can occur when we create new circuits, new pathways in the brain. It is these actual physical changes in our brain's neural structure that make possible new, healthier life habits.

During meditation there is a dramatic increase in the activity of the left side of the prefrontal neocortex of the brain associated with a sense of well-being and the complete absence of anxiety. When you meditate, your brain experiences heightened states of peace and contentment, and as it does so, it begins to change its architecture by rewiring itself around such emotional states. Mindfulness changes lives by changing minds!

The 3Cs is a mindfulness meditation; through it you achieve a state of mind that is calm and stable. "Mindfulness" simply means awareness of the present moment. In meditation, this often means awareness of your own sensations, especially your breath. In the process, your mind becomes cleared of negative, encumbering emotions. You will learn the 3Cs meditation technique in the next chapter. Remember, it must be done every day if it is to work in the process of change. *Change takes practice!*

THE SCREENING ROOM: THE PRACTICE OF CREATING

Once you have engaged the 3Cs to clear your mind, you will be ready to create the future you desire. To do so, you need to discover how to let go of the intellect (with its overcritical and overanalytical cognitive patterns), and to fully engage the subconscious mind in creating the life changes you seek.

I always tell my clients, "Act as if you were, and you will become." As we know from the dream state, the subconscious mind cannot distinguish between what is real and what is vividly imagined. The second stage of the Fresh Start program is, therefore, a self-hypnosis practice called the Screening Room. Using this *creative* hypnosis technique, you will generate and envision compelling, vivid images of the specific future you desire. You will rehearse your future as you would like to live it. During this visualization, you will imagine in detail the sights, sounds, and feelings of such a desired future, creating new cognitive impressions that will seed in the subconscious mind. Once they are blueprinted there, you will begin to experience them in your life. *Act as if you were, and you will become!*

Through regular visits to the Screening Room, you will begin to fully imagine the person you would like to be and the life you would like to live. You will create an absolutely compelling vision for change, one so vivid that you will be able to experience it fully in your subconscious, then fully in your life. This is how you will make it real! As Napoleon Hill, founder of the American "philosophy of achievement" movement, reminded us, "Whatever the mind of man can conceive and believe, it can achieve." Hill's approach has recently been compellingly updated and expanded in a book that has swept and sparked the American popular consciousness: Rhonda Byrne's *The Secret*. In this exciting new formulation of the mind's power to change lives, Byrne tells us that first we must ask, believe, receive. To experience change, we must believe we have already received the changes we seek. Change depends on our successfully imagining that the future has already arrived. At the moment we become able to do so, it does so as well. The force at work here is called the law of attraction: like attracts like. While this idea may be challenging, it is also profoundly exciting, for it puts an enormous power within our grasp: once we understand and achieve it, our thoughts begin to alter our reality!

As you spend time in the Screening Room throughout these twenty-eight days, you will be engaging the law of attraction. Using a trained mind and directed thought, you will visualize and experience specifically targeted life changes. In this way, you will create them.

If you are a little worried about engaging in a practice such as self-hypnosis and using the law of attraction, let me put your mind at ease! The practice is effortless, pleasant, and absolutely safe. You will not be giving up control—you will, in fact, be taking control. Through self-hypnosis you will fully tap the creative power of your subconscious mind, now known to be responsible for all deep-rooted and lasting behavioral changes.

The important thing to remember is that the subconscious can only be successfully accessed when imagery is vividly present, when the mind has been calmed, when the brain waves have been slowed to the *alpha* state, where it is receptive and ready to receive new information. Thus you need to regularly practice the 3Cs before visiting the Screening Room!

Your 3Cs and your visits to the Screening Room will go hand in hand. You will need to practice them at least twice a day if new, positive mental reconditioning is to take place. Remember learning to drive a car? At first it took concentration. Over time it became effortless, second nature. So it shall be in your practice of the 3Cs and your visits to the Screening Room.

THE LANGUAGE OF THE HEART

To make sure that this entire process is successful, let us look at one last component: learning the Language of the Heart.

To do so, you first need to become aware of your inner dialogue, the "voices in your head." You have them, do you not? Are they warm, loving, supportive? Or are they the voices of criticism and judgment? With the Language of the Heart, you will subdue and disarm these inner critics. You will turn your critics into coaches. By learning this new language, you will transform your emotions and, in the process, begin to feel worthy of positive life change. You will reclaim your hope, your courage, your enthusiasm! You will take the actions necessary for positive life outcomes.

. . . .

This chapter has revealed the importance of changing the mind. Now let's illustrate it with an extended visual metaphor, so prepare to open your mind. Get ready to stretch that imagination way, way out there. I would like you to view your mind as your house! Work with me here, okay? If you're familiar with the expression "head space," you'll grasp this quickly.

Let's say you have tried to change in the past, but without much success. As a result of these past failures, maybe you have concluded that you will never change, that you can never change, that you will be forever cramped into a space that is too small, too limiting: altogether unsatisfactory. So many times you've tried to "renovate" your life to make it better, happier. Always you've ended up back in the same old place, with the same old behaviors, feeling once again that you've failed.

Redesigning your mind and, in turn, your life may require a consultant! This is where I come in, dear reader! I am here to help you create the life you've imagined, to successfully create a new life-space. I am here as your interior designer! This is what I do—what I have been doing for over twenty years now. This is how I've helped hundreds of people reimagine and reinvent their lives! Whenever doubt arises, I will be here to offer the new tools, the new vision, and the new language you need for successful life change.

So before we begin our practical hands-on work in the next chapter, let's walk through the important rooms and features of your existing mental space. Are you ready for a tour of your mind?

Let's first step into the *living room*, the space of conscious awareness. Notice that it is filled with fixtures and furniture—these are your thoughts. Some of these furnishings are in dire need of reupholstering, perhaps with brighter, cleaner fabrics, but you know this already. In the next chapter, we will begin to rearrange the furniture, removing some pieces and acquiring new ones: new thoughts. You will engage in some activities that will alter the function of your living room and lead to lasting life change. It is in your living room that you will conduct your daily meditations, where you will develop greater self-awareness, where you will learn to speak the Language of the Heart.

Now follow me down this hidden passageway. It leads to a room you might not even know exists, though it is actually the most powerful room in your house. You are entering the library, your *subconscious library*, a room filled with the record of your life experiences, including all your unproductive memories from the past, all your emotional melodramas. But have a good look around, my friend, for in this room there are also many empty spaces, shelves just waiting to be filled with positive new volumes, inspirational books of empowering new beliefs—new volumes for a new life!

Now look around the corner. Here is a completely empty space in your house: a void. Though there is nothing in this space at present, over the next twenty-eight days you will build a new room here. When it's completed, it will be your *screening room.* This will be your creative space. Here you will imagine, rehearse, and manifest your visions of success.

Okay, now you're working with me! Now you have a sense of your mind's space, of its present conditions, of the renovations required for significant life change. Keep that tour foremost in your mind as you move forward to the next chapter.

Take a moment now to imagine the next twenty-eight days of your life. Picture yourself waking up every morning, opening your eyes, smiling, and saying: "I want to live this day. I am happy to be me." This is how it will go in the Fresh Start program! Are you ready, then, to begin the practice of change?

2

The Practice of Changing Your Mind

Did chapter 1 plant the seeds of possibility? Has it helped you sense that the change you seek must be born of a new understanding, a new orientation? This is my deepest hope! Shall we go forward then and begin the practice of change?

Chapter 2 will take you step by step and day by day through the first week of your Fresh Start. All that is needed now is your commitment to yourself: forty minutes a day—twenty in the morning, twenty at night. Is this too much to ask? I hope not! Remember, *change takes practice*!

If you're really busy, you'll need to get creative to find this time—but do it. And stay with it! At first it may feel like pushing open a heavy, rusted door, a door that hasn't been used in years. Think back; perhaps you remember it. This a door you probably used in childhood. Do you remember now? It led to a garden, and that's where it will begin to take you now . . .

Be prepared. The first push will be tough—perhaps nothing will move at all. The key is repetition. Every time you lean on the door, it will loosen, perhaps imperceptibly at first. But inevitably, the rust that binds the door will begin to flake and fall away. Soon you will see a sliver of light. With your daily practice, this sliver will grow wider and wider. Then one day soon, the door will swing free and you will find yourself standing in a garden of light!

Here is your schedule for the first week of your Fresh Start foundational work. Study it. Follow it. This is the path to change!

The Fresh Start Promise

WEEK ONE DAILY SCHEDULE

DAY 1

Morning
The 3Cs Meditation: An Introduction
  to the Practice of Clearing

Evening
The Language of the Heart
3Cs Meditation Practice

DAY 2

Morning
Fresh Start Question 1
3Cs Meditation Practice

Evening
3Cs Meditation Practice
The Rowboat Meditation

DAY 3

Morning
3Cs Meditation Practice
The Armor of Light Meditation

Evening
3Cs Meditation Practice
Victory Count: Reflect on Your Day
  in a Positive Way

DAY 4

Morning
Fresh Start Question 2
The Screening Room: An
  Introduction to the Practice of
  Creating

Evening
The Screening Room Practice
Victory Count

DAY 5

Morning
3Cs Meditation Practice
Sword of Fearlessness Meditation

Evening
The Screening Room Practice
Victory Count

DAY 6

Morning
Fresh Start Question 3
3Cs Meditation Practice

Evening
3Cs Meditation Practice, followed
  by the Screening Room
Victory Count

DAY 7

Morning
3Cs Meditation Practice
The Horizon Meditation

Evening
3Cs Meditation Practice, with a
  shortcut to the Screening Room
Victory Count

Getting Started

I would like you to find a quiet area to sit in peacefully. Dedicate this space as a place for meditation. You should be comfortable and peaceful here. But know that everything you need is already inside you— above all, your willingness to try something new in your quest for positive change.

Day № 1   Morning

Have you found your place? Good. Let's begin. This morning's practice takes place in your internal living room, the room of conscious awareness. You've heard the expression "Today is the first day of the rest of your life"? Well, guess what? That day has finally arrived! This morning you will learn the 3Cs meditation. These are the Cs:

1. Calm the body

2. Center the mind

3. Connect with the spirit: Put the 3Cs together

The 3Cs Meditation: The Practice of Clearing
TO CALM, CENTER, AND CONNECT

This is a cornerstone of your Fresh Start program, an ongoing practice to clear the mind, making room to create change. With the 3Cs you will calm the body, center the mind, and connect with the spirit.

CALM THE BODY

First let's practice some deep breathing, taking all our breaths through the nose. Take a moment to settle yourself, then follow these steps:

1. Place one hand on your chest and the other on your stomach, chest and shoulders relaxed. Only your belly will move in this exercise.

2. Exhale deeply, letting all the air out.

3. Inhale, and as you do so, imagine that a balloon in your belly is filling with air. As you breathe in, count one, two, three, four.

4. Hold your breath for the count of four.

5. Exhale, deflating the balloon in your belly, this time counting to eight. (If that feels too long at first, start with four and build up gradually as you practice.)

6. Make sure your shoulders are down and your chest relaxed.

7. Repeat the process. Could anything be easier?

As you breathe out, you release tension, stress, and fear. You also exhale warm, "used" air that contains carbon dioxide. Imagine that your lungs are like sponges, and you are squeezing CO_2 out of them with each exhalation.

As you breathe in, your lungs expand, taking in fresh, cool air. Inhaling says yes to new life. The Chinese call this breath *chi*, the energy of life. As your lungs expand and recharge, your body is infused with life energy, with chi.

Visualize all the oxygen in each life-giving breath as the color of sparkling golden light. Visualize the spent air you exhale as a smoky gray cloud. In with the golden light, out with the used gray cloud. Open up your lungs to take in new choices, new opportunities for joy, enthusiasm, and courage. *Change begins with the first breath.*

Are you calm now? Or calmer? Good. Once calm, you can begin to center the mind.

CENTER THE MIND

Centering your mind means quieting the constant chatter that prevents you from feeling strong and grounded. It means clearing away the anxious and critical thoughts that distract you from a lucid vision of your desired future. Your daily practice of calming and centering will restore emotional balance, neutralize your negative energy, and help you regain your true balanced nature.

Let's begin with a simple visualization. Picture your everyday thoughts and emotions as wind-tossed waves that constantly shift and change. But like the ocean's waves, they constitute only the surface of your conscious experience. Underneath is a place of perpetual peace. (In this visualization we will go to that peaceful underwater scene. But if you'd rather not picture yourself underwater, feel free to substitute the image of a serene lake, without a ripple disturbing it, and keep yourself above its surface.)

For a moment, imagine yourself diving beneath the ocean's surface turmoil down to the bright sea floor, where all is calm, all is still. Visualize the beauty of the ocean floor: the sand, the clear water, the fish swimming placidly through the coral. (Do not, please, visualize any sharks! No predators are here, only pearls of joy in the silent depths of your being.) The surface of the mind ripples constantly, but at the deepest levels of your inner spirit is tranquility. The 3Cs meditation will grant you access to your inner peace—and during that time you are free.

Now move on to the following meditation. As you read it, take time to fully absorb the meaning of the words. Don't rush! Pause occasionally to observe what you are feeling. Your Fresh Start is all about awareness. You will start to change your awareness right now.

CONNECT TO THE SPIRIT: PUTTING THE 3CS TOGETHER

The 3Cs meditation practice gives you access to a safe place within. Sit up in a chair now, straighten your spine, and place your feet flat on the floor. Exhale three times through your mouth to release your stress.

Now imagine a golden string pulling you up, connecting your head to the blue sky—the world of infinite possibilities. Imagine roots growing from your feet, or powerful magnets locking your feet to the ground, connecting you to Mother Earth—securing and nurturing.

Notice your breathing. Give your full attention to breathing *out* all the worries and concerns of your day. Place a hand on your belly and notice what happens. Feel your hand drop as you exhale, then rise as you inhale. Notice the continuous flow as your breath *out* becomes your breath *in*. Allow yourself to drift into a quiet calmness inside.

As you breathe out, say to yourself, *Let go.*
As you breathe in, say to yourself, *Calm.*

Continue to repeat *Let go* with the out-breath, *calm* with the in-breath. *Let go. Calm.* Begin to notice that your breath is slowing down more and more, relaxing you more and more. Give yourself permission to release anything in the way of this calming experience.

Now place a smile on your face, letting the corners of your mouth lift toward your ears. This is the *Inner Smile*, an ancient Chinese practice that instills contentment, gratitude, and completion. Do you find it difficult? Remember, change takes practice. Keep trying to cultivate your smile!

Do you have your smile now? Wonderful! Now please smile at this calm, safe moment and declare:

Calm. My mind is like the silent bottom of the sea. No ripples of thought disturb it.

Centered. I breathe and gather all of my energy back into my belly, my sacred power center.

Connected. I am surrounded by a circle of pure light from the sun. This life force connects me to the world of infinite possibilities.

Now begin to notice the balance of energies between the left and right sides of your body. This perception may be elusive at first, so for now just begin to notice. There is a balance to be found here, don't you think? Begin to enjoy its perfect symmetry.

Whenever you need them, whenever you are assailed by disturbances or agitations of the mind, you may use these words: *Calm, centered, connected.* These words are the foundation for all future practice. They will unlock the door to calm. They are your personal combination to deep-rooted change. Repeated over time, they will recondition your mind and its responses. You can use them any place and any time: on the train or the bus, in line at the supermarket. *Calm, centered, connected.*

So put down this book now and go about your day. Try to remember to visit your living room from time to time. Step in and take a seat—this is, after all, *your* room for the practice of the 3Cs. Take your deep calming breaths and use that word combination: *Calm, centered, and connected*. From a place of balance and calm, all possibilities, actions, and positive emotions become open to you.

Day №1   Evening

How did your first day go? Did you remember to visit your living room? Perhaps you entirely forgot about the 3Cs! Either way, it's okay. Over time you will begin to use this meditation during the day, to realize its value, its power to create change. You will return to the 3Cs tonight, but first, some food for thought. Here what you will focus on this evening:

1. The Language of the Heart

2. 3Cs Meditation Practice

We'll begin with a story.

The Cherokee Parable of the Two Wolves

One evening an old Cherokee told his grandson about an ancient battle—a never-ending conflict that goes on still. He said, "My son, inside us there is a battle, a war between the two wolves that inhabit us all. Inside one wolf is anger, envy, jealousy, sadness, regret, greed, arrogance, self-pity. Inside the other is joy, peace, love, hope, serenity, humility, kindness, benevolence, compassion."

The grandson considered the elder's words for a moment. It seemed true, what the grandfather said, yet he was troubled by one question. Raising his eyes to meet the old man's, he asked: "Grandfather, which wolf wins?"

The old Cherokee smiled at the question and then replied simply, "The one you feed the most."

The Language of the Heart

Most of us are very self-critical. We are our own worst enemies. We think we should be more successful, more beautiful, more accomplished, more intelligent, more *this*, more *that*. We carry shame, guilt, and a poor self-image from childhood into our adult lives. We employ them in constant judgment of our failures and shortcomings. In other words, we feed the wrong wolf. The unhappy, critical wolf grows stronger while the wolf who would be happy, loving, and satisfied grows weaker and weaker. This must change!

Why do we feed the wrong wolf? Why can't we defend ourselves against that enemy that has been called the "inner critic"? Why do we accept from ourselves the harsh judgment we would likely not accept from anyone else? The reason is devastatingly simple: this, for many of us, is the only language we know. It is stored in the old, toxic books and recordings in our subconscious library. It is the language we learned as children, then, disastrously, became fluent in as adults.

Now is the time to change all that, but it will take time and practice. First, you need to become more aware of the old critical voices. To hear them distinctly, in all their toxicity and judgment. To recognize them for what they are, a foreign and acidic tongue. Once you recognize them, you will begin to see that you have a choice in the words you use. There is another language out there, you know, one that is quite sweet and beautiful to the ear! It is called the Language of the Heart.

It all begins with love. This is a language based on the revolutionary idea that when you treat your own self as a friend, as a loved one, you cultivate emotional balance and prosperity. Can you learn to speak to yourself with support and understanding? It may be a strange concept at first! You can start by avoiding all those negative labels, the *should nots, have nots, cannots, must nots.* Instead, begin to use and favor *I choose, I give myself permission, I am willing, I can.*

As we begin to practice the Language of the Heart by avoiding the negatives, we often encounter resistance. We seem to prefer the old and familiar language. As we learn this new one, we may often slip back into those well-established behaviors. Here is a technique to use when you catch yourself being self-critical: first, reestablish awareness of the old voice, that foreign and toxic tongue. You might even picture yourself feeding the unhappy wolf—watch him hungrily chomping! Then, without any judgment whatsoever, say the word *cancel*. This word interrupts the pattern. It clears the cluttered screen of the present moment. Then, on the fresh, blank screen, write some loving words instead—feed the other wolf!

Or consider another ritual, even more powerful. This one may strike you as completely over the top—if it does, if it makes you squirm in discomfort, note your unease and know that you are probably one of the people most in need of such loving work!

In my own life, when I have completed a seminar or any other difficult challenge, I take myself aside for a little *tète a tète*, an inner dialogue, a love fest! I usually tell myself something like this: "Edwige, you are simply amazing. I have to hand it to you. To speak before all these people you don't know, and to look so confident and at ease. I am proud of you, woman! You did a great job, and you know what, each time you do this, you get better!" Giving yourself some love feels good, but more importantly, it creates new, positive volumes in your subconscious library. And guess what? Once the new and loving Language of the Heart is permanently recorded in the library, it begins to get airplay. As you replay it, learning its lovely cadences and harmonies, it begins to rise in the charts of your consciousness, becoming more and more popular with its audience. Why wouldn't it? Such language is sweetness to the ear! You will begin to request it more, to use it more often. In response to its popularity, new recordings will be made, stored, and played back. The number of Language of the Heart recordings will soon equal the old "hits" and eventually outnumber them. The old songs of doubt and criticism will lie idle, gathering dust. Eventually—and this will be a sweet day indeed—such language will become a dead and forgotten tongue, abandoned forever. So begin to record! Begin to practice the Language of the Heart.

The 3Cs Meditation Practice

Practice the 3Cs meditation—yes, again! Reread it first to refresh your memory: see pages 32–35. If your mind starts to wander (as it may), bring it back without judgment, without exasperation. Remember, each time you practice, you become better. Be persistent! Afterwards, re-focus on your breath. Notice any sensations you feel and continue to breathe peacefully. Carry the awareness of the 3Cs into the world with you. If you become uncomfortable, agitated, or annoyed, don't give up. The 3Cs are essential, the ABCs of change. Keep at it!

Day №2   Morning

Throughout the program of change, you'll be answering nine "Fresh Start Questions"—beginning today. Your two activities for this morning are:

1. Fresh Start Question 1

2. 3Cs Meditation Practice

Fresh Start Question 1

Magically, the act of writing can itself bring forth new ideas. Therefore, don't simply read this exercise and skip the writing part. Please write! Your insights will be different, more powerful, if you sit quietly and write down your thoughts.

The first question:

What do I desire to change about my life in twenty-eight days?

It may take five seconds for you to write, "I want to lose eight to ten pounds," but don't stop there. Ask yourself why this goal is important to you. What are your private reasons for having this desire? Since the Fresh Start program is about changing from the inside out, you need to make a strong connection with your inner motivation for change. In this example, if your motivation is "everyone else thinks I'm too heavy," it is rooted in the negative. If, on the other hand, your motivation is "I can't wait to feel better—and to fit into those pants!" you'll be connected to a positive incentive for change.

So take a minute now to write down your response to this question. (You can write down several, then choose one.) Think of a goal with an emotional resonance: when you contemplate it, it fills you with joy. And make your goal specific and concrete: not "I want to be happy" but

"I want to finish my degree." Make it a positive construction: "I want to be thin" instead of "I don't want to be overweight." Finally, make it an important goal. Take a chance! Select one of those "breakthrough" goals that often leads to other accomplishments. Losing weight is a good example, because it will likely lead to other goals, better health, perhaps finding a mate, and so on.

The 3Cs Meditation Practice

Although you are doing this meditation for only the third time, you are probably beginning to get the hang of it. (Reread pages 32–35 to refresh your memory.) If your mind wants to think about all the things you have to do today, gently return yourself to your meditation. You can think about your busy day later!

Tip of the Day
ENCOURAGING WORDS

Last night, you had your first lesson in the Language of the Heart. As you live your day today, remember to use positive and encouraging words with yourself and others. The wolf who would be happy could use a meal! Feed that wolf with the food of happiness. And one more thing: remember to smile! Even if it doesn't come easily, keep cultivating that smile!

Day №2   Evening

How did your day go today? Did you practice the 3Cs when things got a little rough, a little storm-tossed? Great! This will eventually become automatic, a reflex that kicks in every time you encounter a disturbance in the waters. Did you practice your new language? Even a few kind words are a beginning. Keep trying. Soon the words will come easier, soon they will join to become phrases, then whole sentences. Fluency in a new language takes time.

Your exercises for tonight are:

1. 3Cs Meditation Practice

2. The Rowboat Meditation

These activities will be calming. Tonight you will use a new progression: after you practice the 3Cs, you will add another meditation.

The 3Cs Meditation Practice

You can do this meditation any time in the evening. Some people use it as a transition between workday and home life; some use it at bedtime. Choose a time when you are not too tired and other people are not clamoring for your attention. Use the 3Cs now, and when you have calmed and cleared your mind, proceed to the Rowboat visualization below.

The Rowboat Meditation
TO LET GO OF WORRIES

Imagine it is a sparkling summer day. You are in a boat on a peaceful lake. It could be a kayak, canoe, rowboat, small sailboat, any boat you like. Look around you. Visualize the details: a blue sky reflects on the surface of the waters, a light breeze cools your face and gently moves the leaves of the trees on the shore. The lake is crystal clear with a sandy bottom.

You want to take your boat out to explore the lake, but your boat is slow and heavy because, as you now notice, it is filled with bags, boxes, and packages.

Pick up the bag that is filled with today's anxieties. Take a moment to say goodbye to them, then toss the bag overboard. Does it sink like a stone, or float away behind you?

Your boat moves a little faster now, but still it is heavy. You realize that you have the perfect opportunity to unburden yourself further, so you pick up a box of worries and throw it overboard. You begin to move more swiftly now.

Continue to throw your concerns into the water. As you do so, your boat lightens until it is gliding effortlessly across the water. You breathe deeply, taking in the clean, fresh air. You feel the sun on your head and listen to the water lapping gently against the hull.

It feels good to release these burdens, doesn't it? Your body feels different. Your shoulders and neck feel looser. Don't you feel lighter? Don't you feel more relaxed, energetic, hopeful? Take a moment to memorize these sensations of clarity and optimism.

Declare to yourself:

I am letting go, trusting in a higher plan that is unfolding for me.

When you are ready, head back to shore. Know that at any time you can take your boat out again and return to this feeling of well-being.

· · · · · · · · · · · · · · · ·

The 3Cs meditation followed by the Rowboat is a wonderfully calming and lightening combination for the evening.

Day №3   Morning

Bonjour! Good morning! Welcome back. You are almost halfway through the first week of your Fresh Start. This morning you will do your clearance with the 3Cs, then, like last evening, you will build on that with a meditation. This one will give you balance, strength, and invincibility for your day:

1. 3Cs Meditation Practice
2. The Armor of Light Meditation

The 3Cs Meditation Practice

This is only your third day of this "clearance" meditation, but by now your practice should be strengthening and its language should be becoming familiar. You may start to notice the calming benefits of this practice that is so essential to well-being. After you have cleared your worries with the 3Cs, go straight into the meditation below.

The Armor of Light Meditation
TO CREATE A CIRCLE OF PROTECTION

Imagine you are surrounded by a circle of divine, sparkling white light that protects you like a warrior's shield. This light penetrates each and every cell of your body—your blood cells, your muscles, your organs, your bones, your skin. The light brings you a sense of absolute well-being, restoring your balance and deflecting negative energy from you. Only God and godly things can enter your life now. You are protected.

Put a little smile on your face to appreciate this experience. Send that smiling energy down to your belly. Remember that this is the center of your courage, strength, and will. To activate this power center, cover your belly with the bright yellow light of the sun. Think to yourself:

I can. I create. I manifest.

Now bring your smiling energy up to your heart center. Remember that this is the center of your joy, compassion, and kindness. To activate it, cover your chest with the green light of the meadows. Think to yourself:

I embrace life with honesty and love.

Now bring your smiling energy up to the middle of your forehead. Remember that this is the center for wisdom, guidance, and intuition. To activate it, cover your forehead with the purple light of amethyst. Think to yourself:

I trust that I will be guided toward my highest good and purpose.

Now that you have activated each center with your attention and smiling energy, take a moment to bask in the light that protects you. Think to yourself:

I feel the light surrounding me now.
It serves as a shield of protection.
Only good and loving things are coming into my life.
With intention and conviction, I reject all negativity.

Tip of the Day

THE POWER OF LANGUAGE

Remember to keep using positive language today and to listen to your inner coach encouraging you. As the Buddha said, "Whatever words we utter should be chosen with care, for people will hear them and be influenced by them for good or ill."

Day №3   Evening

How was your day? Did you enjoy some purposefulness? Did you generate courage with the Armor of Light? Did you feed the happy wolf?

Your activities for tonight are:

1. 3Cs Meditation Practice

2. Victory Count: Reflect on your day in a positive way

On the third day of your Fresh Start program, you are already learning to clear your mind. You are using the Language of the Heart to begin to silence your inner critic and encourage your inner coach. You are throwing your worries overboard and protecting yourself with the Armor of Light. Now you will learn how to look for opportunities and reinforce change by reviewing events at the end of each day.

The 3Cs Meditation Practice

This meditation is essential to the success of the program because it lets you clear your mind's chatter and find your inner place of peace. At first, you will simply notice the relief of feeling calm. In time, as you continue to sit in your quiet living room, the room of conscious awareness, you will discover your true inner nature and authentic self.

Victory Count
REFLECT ON YOUR DAY IN A POSITIVE WAY

In chapter 1 you learned about the importance of re-recording the old volumes in your subconscious library. One way to do this is to deliberately try new things and cultivate successful experiences every day. These experiences may be large and impressive, or they may be little things no one else notices. What matters is that they are changing your expectations about what you can accomplish.

At the end of your day, sit quietly and reflect on everything that happened. Make a point of experiencing gratitude for the things that went right. Even if you had a bad day, you can find something to appreciate. If you are feeling cranky, keep reflecting on your day until you feel a little ember of gratitude. Continue to place grateful thoughts on this ember until it sparks a flame of thankfulness.

Here is your practice: as you review your day, notice the victories, large or small, and write them down. What did you accomplish? Did you say or do anything differently? The process of writing down your accomplishments creates a positive record of your progress, and it trains you to be more observant.

Do not beat yourself up if you feel you could have handled something better. Perhaps you fell victim to the dessert tray. You'd planned to say no, but you couldn't resist. But perhaps the good news is that you didn't eat the whole thing! Or you stopped at just one serving! There's your victory! Instead of judging yourself for eating the dessert in the first place, celebrate whatever accomplishment you can find in it. Accentuate the positive and find evidence of success. It's there if you look for it.

Day №4   Morning

Today is a big day! Now that you are more comfortable with the 3Cs meditation, which you use to *clear* your mind, it's time to learn the second step, which you use to *create* the future you desire.

Your activities for this morning are:

1. Fresh Start Question 2
2. The Screening Room self-hypnosis technique

Fresh Start Question 2

Again, even if you're busy, *write down* your responses to get the full benefit of this question. New thoughts will surface as you write.

The second question is:

How will I know when I reach my desired goal?

I know it's possible to answer this question in one sentence, but that would defeat the purpose of this exercise, which is to create a vivid picture of your success. Let's say you want a new job. You'll know you have reached your goal when the job is yours. But you'll also have a new workplace, a new commute, a new boss and co-workers, new responsibilities. You might wear different clothes, or even live in a new city. What will be the indicators of your success? How will you look and feel? What will other people say? Write down all your responses in detail because you will need them in the next activity.

Remember, the ideal answer is very specific. You should be able to see or clearly sense that indicator of success. Your answer should also have a strong emotion attached to it, like the exuberant feeling that accompanies a promotion or a new relationship.

The Screening Room: The Practice of Creating

In the 3Cs meditation, you cleared your mind. Here in the Screening Room, you will create: you will vividly imagine your new life as you are achieving your desired goal. On an ongoing basis, you will practice your new future by creating a mental movie of what it will look, feel, sound, and even smell like! Your movie will be composed of all the specific details of your answer to Fresh Start Question 2.

As we noted in chapter 1, you need not be apprehensive about self-hypnosis. It is just a way to experience thoughts, feelings, and images as visualized reality. It helps install new mental software, reprogramming your subconscious mind to create the future you desire.

Read "The Screening Room" three times before trying it for the first time. You may want to refer to it before your next visits to the Screening Room, but eventually you won't need to read it at all before entering. Instead of popcorn, take your answers to Fresh Start Question 2 with you.

The Screening Room Practice
TO CREATE THE FUTURE YOU DESIRE

1. Sit comfortably and begin by looking up at the ceiling. Take three or four deep breaths to help you relax. Say to yourself, preferably aloud:

   As I watch this spot on the ceiling, my eyelids will become heavier and heavier. Soon they will be so heavy that they will close, and I will be in a state of hypnosis.

2. Repeat that phrase a few times until you feel your eyes wanting to close. As your eyes close, say to yourself:

   Relax now ... let go ... deeper now.
   Relax now ... let go ... deeper now.
   Relax now ... let go ... deeper now.

3. Begin to explore the sensations of your body. Feel your shoulders letting go of tensions, your arms feeling heavy, your legs feeling loose
and limp. Gradually your body is becoming totally relaxed.

4. You are now ready for a deeper state of hypnosis. Say to yourself:

> **Now I am going deeper and deeper . . .**
> **Now I am going deeper and deeper . . .**
> **Now I am going deeper and deeper . . .**

Continue to repeat this phrase until you experience what you are
telling yourself.

5. Then imagine yourself standing at the top of a five-step staircase.
Now descend the steps, counting backward from five to one. As you
do so, you are reaching a peaceful and very safe place.

6. At the bottom of the staircase there is a hallway. As you walk down
this hallway you discover a door marked "Screening Room." Imagine yourself entering this room, where you see a comfortable chair
facing a big movie screen. The moment you sit in that chair you
become the scriptwriter, director, and star of your own show. Take
time to project in detail the scene that illustrates your desired goal.
See yourself doing what you want to do, being the way you want to
be. Let yourself fully experience the feeling of success and joy.

   As you watch your movie on the screen, say to yourself out loud:

> **I _choose_ to have this experience.**
> **I _can_ have this experience.**
> **I am now _creating_ this experience _every day in every way._**

7. Take time to savor this moment. To anchor it at your body's cellular
level, I suggest you make a fist with your nondominant hand and repeat three times aloud: "Victory to me. Victory is mine." Know that
you will return to your usual activities with a sense of emotional,
mental, and physical balance. Put a smile on your face as a sign of
deep appreciation.

8. Get ready now to return from this hypnosis experience, feeling re-freshed, excited, and expecting to have the results that you desire. Imagine walking back down the hallway to the stairs. Walk up the steps, counting from one to five. When you reach number five, open your eyes and smile.

. . . .

How did you do? Remember, this was your first time. Although you may not have reached the deepest stages of hypnosis, today you made an important beginning in this essential Fresh Start technique. Soon you will become more skillful in your use of the Screening Room. Over time, you will learn to recondition the mind at the deepest levels in the process of life change.

As you go about your day today, keep in mind this image of your success. From time to time, use your anchor: make a fist with your non-dominant hand and declare (preferably aloud): "Victory to me. Victory is mine." Every time you repeat this exercise you will reinforce the experience and help create your desired outcome.

Day № 4   Evening

How was your day? Were you more encouraging and loving to your-self? Are you breathing more deeply, feeling more in touch with your power center (your belly), gathering your strength and peaceful energy? Are you feeling more centered within? Did you appreciate your armor's protection?

Your two activities for this evening are:

1. The Screening Room Practice

2. Victory Count: Reflect on your day in a positive way

The Screening Room Practice

Remember, the mind cannot distinguish between what is real and what is vividly imagined, so what you imagine can make as powerful an impression on your subconscious mind as real events.

The Screening Room helps you develop positive expectations. This is important because your expectations will be fulfilled. If disaster is all you can imagine, then disaster is what you will create! On the other hand, visualizing what you desire and imagine to be possible helps create a positive outcome.

Reread this technique: see pages 32–35. Try to memorize it, and practice it again, adding more details to your home movie. Go easy on yourself if you forget some of the language. The three key phrases to remember are *Relax, Let go,* and *Deeper now.*

Victory Count

REFLECT ON YOUR DAY IN A POSITIVE WAY

What are you grateful for today? What went right? What did you do well? Did you experience any successes or victories? Were you able to accentuate the positive in a difficult situation? What steps did you take toward your desired goal? Thinking about the experiences of your day and placing them in context gives them added significance. Write them down as a concrete reminder, if you wish.

Day №5   Morning

Bonjour! You have only two more days left in the first week of your Fresh Start. Victory to you! This morning you have another treat in store: a new visualization. Your two activities are:

1. 3Cs Meditation Practice

2. The Sword of Fearlessness Meditation

As always, keep a positive attitude today by using the Language of the Heart and listening to your inner coach. Make some new recordings. Remember to visualize success!

The 3Cs Meditation Practice

Today, begin with the 3Cs to calm, center, and connect, then move straight into the Sword of Fearlessness.

The Sword of Fearlessness Meditation
TO DEVELOP STRENGTH AND COURAGE

Sit comfortably and breathe deeply. Be clear.

Imagine you are in an outdoor space, perhaps a forest. You are standing erect, legs, trunk, and feet firmly rooted to the earth. It is a warm and sunny day, with an invigorating breeze blowing. Your body is alert but relaxed, and your mind is free. You are untroubled.

Conjure up a specific goal, one that fear has prevented you from achieving, one that still must be accomplished. Perhaps it is a difficult but necessary phone call you have been putting off, or a conversation with a friend, colleague, or boss. It might be a difficult meeting you need to initiate.

Now visualize yourself approaching the scene of that future event with a sword of light in your hand. Look at your sword. It is magnificent. Its blade shines in the sun and as you move forward it reflects brilliant rays of powerful light. Have fun with this. Perhaps you are King Arthur or Xena the Warrior Princess. Feel how purposeful you are now that you have the power of fearlessness in your hand.

What is your intention? Think again about your goal. Take the energy of the sun and the sword and transform it into the energy of absolute conviction. Feel your courage and resilience. It is now within your capacity to move forward to the destiny of this event with clarity and confidence. All fear and doubt have been banished.

Declare to yourself:

My breath is calm and effortless.
I breathe into my belly, my power center.
I feel my strength, my courage.
I feel unstoppable.
I am ready to act.
I can, I do, I will.

. . . .

Know now that the strength you have manifested with the sword of fearlessness is rooted in a power that is already yours. You have always had it. It shall always be available to you. When meddling fears diminish your energy, return to this image of you and the sword and the sun. Reach for your power by reaching for this image. You are unstoppable.

My client Adele could not stop eating that pint of ice cream every night as she watched *Law and Order,* her favorite TV show. She used to feel powerless and disgusted with herself for being unable to resist this little routine. I told her to have fun, if she wanted to, and imagine herself as a warrior with a sword of fearlessness. If the pint of ice cream came too close, the sword would pierce and destroy that pint container. Adele laughed deliciously, thinking this was absolutely far-fetched, but a few days later she told me that it actually worked! She could watch her show in peace, feeling proud of her new behavior. Using the image of the sword helped Adele interrupt a habitual pattern—and anger was replaced by delight.

Tip of the Day
POSITIVE ATTITUDE

As always, keep a positive attitude by using the Language of the Heart. Remember, you have a sword at your side and a happy wolf to feed. If you find yourself with time on your hands, take that boat out on the lake. (See the Rowboat meditation on Day Two.) And remember, visualize success! Victory to you!

Day №5   Evening

Bonsoir! Did you do something courageous today? Perhaps you enjoyed a different perspective. Did this change your experience of the day? I hope so!

Your two activities for this evening are:

1. The Screening Room Practice

2. Victory Count: Reflect on your day in a positive way

Today you will further strengthen your practice: repetition creates reconditioning. Remember, *change takes practice!*

Have you heard the story about a young man who went in search of a particular enlightened master? He went from town to town until someone pointed out an old man. The seeker went to him and asked the master, "What did you do before your enlightenment?"

The master replied, "Chopped wood and carried water from the well."

"And now that you have become enlightened, what do you do now?"

The master replied, "Chop wood and carry water."

The seeker was troubled by this. Puzzled, he asked, "But what has changed, then?"

The master answered, "The difference is on the inside. Before, I was doing everything in my sleep. Now I am awake. The world is still the same, yet I have changed; therefore the world is different for me."

With your daily practice, you are developing a new awareness, the beginnings of a master's enlightenment. You will begin to feel different doing the same things. Your inner life will start to change. Such changes will be evident in the Screening Room. With each visit, the projected pictures and feelings of visualized change will become more vivid and real to you. In time, they will become you.

The Screening Room Practice

This will be your third visit to the Screening Room. Trust in your ability to engage fully in this practice.

Victory Count

REFLECT ON YOUR DAY IN A POSITIVE WAY

As you have done before, take a moment to recall the positive experiences you had today. Write them down.

Day №6   Morning

Bonjour! You have only one day left in your first week! Today is mastery day!

Here are your two activities:

1. Fresh Start Question 3

2. 3Cs Meditation Practice

Fresh Start Question 3

Remember, write your answers down: it greatly enriches your thought process. Here is your third question:

How will my life be different after I reach my goal?

In Question 1 you defined what you wanted to change, and in Question 2 you listed the specific indicators of that change. Now you will take this process to the next level. What other positive outcomes will be generated by your change? The larger repercussions? Now that you have energy, momentum, courage, and optimism, what else will you do? For example, if you chose to lose eight to ten pounds this month, you are gaining momentum and your energy is spiraling upward, boosting your self-esteem. Become aware that if you can achieve this goal, nothing can prevent you from even greater life change. You will do more with greater ease, day after day. You will begin to dare to reach for other, greater goals.

As usual, let your answer have both a physical and an emotional component. It will help if you can both *see* and *feel* the impact of reaching this goal as well as its effects on your relationships, career, social life, and so on.

The 3Cs Meditation Practice

By now you know the 3Cs by heart. Your mind and body will soon begin to seek the peace of this essential practice. Perhaps they have already. The more you use the Cs, the better you will feel. They can be used any place, any time, without disturbing anyone. There will be no "rebound" or side effects—except for boundless energy, enthusiasm, and joy.

Tip of the Day

ENVISION YOUR FUTURE

As you start this new day, remember to use positive and encouraging language with yourself and others. Give yourself credit for any successes you experience today, and hold a picture in your mind of the future you desire.

Day №6   Evening

Bonsoir! Your two activities for this evening are:

1. 3Cs Meditation Practice, followed by the Screening Room

2. Victory Count: Reflect on your day in a positive way

Remember, you are in training now. You are developing self-discipline. Daily repetition is necessary for conditioning. You are becoming like a tennis player who practices every day without complaining: he knows that practice is the only way to develop the ease, confidence, and physical conditioning he needs to become a champion.

The 3Cs Practice, followed by the Screening Room

Now that you have been practicing Fresh Start techniques for six days, do you notice any further resistance about continuing? The mind does not like change. You know this because in the past you have tried to change, but without lasting success. Be patient—this time you are recording new volumes in your subconscious library; this time you are reconditioning the mind. This time, it's different!

Victory Count
REFLECT ON YOUR DAY IN A POSITIVE WAY

Every evening you have an opportunity to celebrate your accomplishments and to see your life in a new light. Are any new patterns emerging? What is becoming easier? What is giving you new pleasure? Remember, writing down your observations will deepen your reflection, deepen your sense of accomplishment and change.

Day № 7   Morning

Today you will again follow the 3Cs meditation with the Screening Room. Used together, these practices create the two-step *clear* and *create* process at the heart of your Fresh Start program.

This morning's activities:

1. 3Cs Meditation Practice, followed by the Screening Room

2. The Horizon Meditation

The 3Cs Practice, followed by the Screening Room

By now this key practice is becoming more automatic. Some days will, of course, be easier than others. Are there days when you feel crazy and unable to sit quietly? Remember, on those days you need these practices the most!

The Horizon Meditation
TO DEVELOP INNER STRENGTH

Imagine you are climbing a rock face just beneath the summit of a mountain. The climb requires some strategy and effort, but you can handle it. You are agile. Your breathing is deep and steady. Feel the strength of your arms and legs, your fingers on the rocks. You are full of enthusiastic purpose.

You look down. Far below you see pine trees. You look up. You see the top of the cliff and clear blue sky above. You clip your harness a little tighter and keep moving.

You know you can do this, and your intention is clear. Imagine energy flowing from your heart into your muscles, linking your heart with your power. You move easily along your heart's path. Whatever you need comes easily to you. Nothing stops you.

Your fingers are strong as they grip the rock. You feel the power of your leg muscles as they push you up the face. You are approaching the top now. With a final push, you are up and over the edge.

Now you are standing on the mountaintop, the world at your feet. The air is crystal clear. You can see farther and wider than you ever imagined. You look out at the horizon and see your future. What is it? What do you see? How do you feel?

Declare to yourself:

I choose to have the best future I can imagine. To make this future real, I pursue it with all my heart, I do the best I can with what I know, and I keep my focus on the outcome.

Know that you have the strength and purpose to attain the future you desire. Any time you feel uncertain, you can return to your heart's path.

. . . .

This motivating exercise is a great way to start your day. It will help you develop perseverance—especially useful when you feel discouraged or when resistance surfaces and you run the risk of sabotaging your own efforts. It will reaffirm the purpose of the journey and help you focus on the outcome. Unlike the Screening Room, which you use to set specific goals, the Horizon visualization strengthens your life's purpose and its course, reinforcing your conviction that you have a mission to accomplish.

Day №7   Evening

Congratulations! You have reached the conclusion of the first week of your Fresh Start. Now that you have learned how to put this week's activities together, here's what you will do this evening:

1. 3Cs Meditation Practice, with a shortcut to the Screening Room

2. Victory Count: Reflect on your day in a positive way

Sometimes you will want to use the 3Cs meditation by itself to simply clear your mind. Or you may want to use the Screening Room by itself to rehearse and visualize your successful day. Either way, these two activities are powerful. When you practice them both twice a day, new mental conditioning takes root in your subconscious library. With practice, you will find refreshment in the calm moments with these techniques. Think about learning to drive a car. At first you had to concentrate. Over time, driving became effortless, second nature. People who meditate regularly often say that with practice, they can shift into absolute calm effortlessly, anywhere, anytime!

The 3Cs Practice, with a shortcut to the Screening Room

Now that you know what it is like to meditate, you may want to get some accessories, like a comfortable cushion to sit on or incense to burn. (Incense is useful because it "watches the clock" for you: when the stick finishes burning, your time is up!) Some people like to wear a shawl while they meditate, partly because it's cozy and partly because it becomes an aspect of the ritual, reminding your body, mind, and spirit that it is time to become calm, centered, connected.

From now on, when you go straight from the 3Cs into the Screening Room, know that you can take a shortcut. You can skip the deep relaxation at the start of the Screening Room practice, because after your 3Cs, you are already relaxed. After repeating calm, centered, connected, keep your eyes closed, go straight to the top of the steps in the Screening Room, and proceed from there, counting from five down to one.

This format is useful for setting daily objectives. For example, let's say you are preparing for a job interview and feel nervous, or you are going to a party and you don't know anyone who will be there. In your Screening Room, imagine a spectacular interview, or a fabulous time mingling at the party. You are getting the idea, I hope! *Visualizing success creates success!*

So go straight from the 3Cs into your Screening Room! Visualize success. As I often tell my students, "Vision, victory, voilà!"

Victory Count
REFLECT ON YOUR DAY IN A POSITIVE WAY

I hope this has now become a regular part of your evening rituals, like brushing your teeth or walking the dog. Chronicle the day's successes now!

Week №1 Wrap-up

Congratulations! You have successfully completed the first week of your program! You have installed the foundation of lasting life change: *clear* (with the 3Cs) and *create* (in your Screening Room). You have begun a momentous journey!

Can you honestly say that you feel the same way you felt a week ago? Aren't you more motivated, more willing to venture into unknown territories these days? I bet you are! Perhaps you are even beginning to feel unstoppable! Wonderful! You may notice a weakening of your old conditioning, and maybe you are kinder to yourself. You should be finding it easier to say no to the old ways, finding that you are much more willing to embrace new life. Doesn't it feel great to have the freedom to make healthy life choices? This is just the beginning, dear reader! I cannot wait to share with you the many secrets of the second week of your Fresh Start! Victory to you!

WEEK TWO
THE BODY

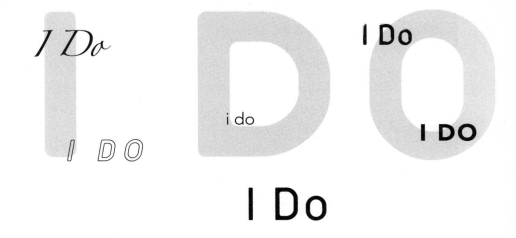

To keep the body in good health is a duty.
Otherwise we shall not be able to keep
our mind strong and clear.
BUDDHA

Every man is the builder of a temple
called his body, nor can he get off by
hammering marble instead.
HENRY DAVID THOREAU

The body says what words cannot.
MARTHA GRAHAM

A healthy mind in a healthy body.
JUVENAL

3

Making Your Body Your Friend

WORK WITH THE BODY: THE MIND WILL FOLLOW

By completing Week One of your Fresh Start, you have taken the first steps along a path to personal transformation! This is a journey—you see that now, I hope—perhaps the greatest journey possible, probably the only one worth making. Let me salute you, then, dear reader. Let me recognize you and celebrate with you these steps you've taken along your rightful path. By making your Fresh Start Promise, you have definitively said yes to yourself. You have embarked upon a practical, time-tested program of life renewal. What a brave and inspired thing to do! Congratulations on your decision. Congratulations for taking the specific actions to move beyond the ordinary, for taking the steps that will help you transcend the merely tolerable. Victory to you, dear reader!

We turn now to the domain of the body, for it is through the agency of the body that you will take the next steps on your journey to transformation and personal victory.

In our desire for life change, most of us seek to include and to change our bodies. There is nothing wrong with this, of course. To exclude our bodily self from our list of desired life changes would be to leave out a significant part of who we are, since we are, after all, a physical being. Clearly, any program of meaningful life change must include the body. Yet when addressing the body, how many of us think exclusively of weight loss and an improved body image? This preoccupation is natural, of course, for we are bombarded daily by images of physically perfect human bodies. But the fact of the matter is that many fall victim to this super-abundance of "body-perfect" imagery. Many of my clients have body issues. Some feel betrayed, some feel oppressed, some feel embarrassed—almost all suffer under the burden of the idea that their bodies are not right, that they are not as they should be, that for them to be happy, they too must become lean and sculpted. In my work with these people who suffer from unhappy relationships with their bodies, it has become clear that their burden is not purely a manifestation of the individual psyche: in fact, it arises from the pressures of membership in the larger collective.

My work with clients has shown me that the body obsession and the diets are almost always a fight against the evil of calories, a part of a much larger war waged against the "sin" of emotional eating. For all its fervor and positive intent, there is little room here for healthfulness or wellness of the spirit. Is health even a goal here? Or is this simply an ongoing, amplified struggle of vanity against the enemy of advancing age?

Our options are limited too, it would seem. Those of us who are simply too disconcerted by the idea of rigorous exercise, or too intimidated by the gym scene, sit on the sidelines feeling left out, feeling bad that we are doing nothing about our bodies. And those of us who choose to do something about our bodies sign up and join the millions who have already succumbed to the allure of the body-perfect American dream. Yet by doing so, how many of us have fallen victim to the extremes of body and the body workout? In my own desire for life change I once became exactly such a victim.

In the early 1990s, I was earning almost my entire living in the fitness world. The gym had been rising to prominence in the American popular lifestyle, and I must have been one of its first true zealots. Teaching twenty hours a week, I offered aerobics with emphasis on body toning, dance, or aquacise; I led stretch and other exercise programs; I was a personal trainer. I was a leading proponent of the lean, muscular body. In those days, I couldn't be thin or trim enough. I worked out before classes, between classes, and after classes, always pushing for greater results. Another hour on the Stairmaster? Wonderful! More weight training? Some more stretching? Excellent! What could be better? I filled my days with disciplined, rigorous exercise. I became thin, fit, and flexible. I was, I thought, the very model of physical fitness.

But one day the extremity of my quest caught up with me, nearly crippling me. I was exercising alone, about halfway through a complex, improvised dance workout, my back arched, my arms extended. The next thing I knew, I was flat on my back, staring at the ceiling, unable to move, hardly able to breathe. One moment I was one of the "fittest" beings on the planet, a leader in this newly popular field. The next moment I lay nearly fully paralyzed on the floor.

Somehow, after an hour on my back, I managed to get up. I cancelled the rest of my classes and, almost literally, crawled home. For a month all I could do was stay absolutely still. An hour on my feet felt heroic to me. I was almost entirely immobilized. What had happened, I wondered? How had I gone from full fitness to full disability? The answer, when I finally accepted it, was simple. In my quest for perfection, I had so taxed my physical resources that my body had finally and definitely said "Enough!"

In the years that followed, I learned that my experience was not so unusual. Again and again, I saw people whose commitment to physical fitness was so complete, so rigorous, that it led them inevitably to physical deterioration. Their workouts were often severe enough to impress the most zealous medieval flagellants: fibers were torn, abs were crunched, muscles aggressively shaped, contoured, and molded. What was at work here? I came to ask. How could this positive desire for fitness produce strain and disability instead? Eventually, after careful observation, I found my answer. In so many, the desire for physical wellbeing was rooted in a singular concern with the body's appearance, its physicality. I was no different, of course. I myself wanted to be thinner, slimmer, sleeker. Yet as we vigorously crafted our bodies to make them more attractive, we often ended up doing more harm than good. Hoping and expecting to feel better about ourselves by transforming our bodily surfaces, how many of us, in fact, have moved further from true physical health? Our bodies are an integral part of our overall being: a truth that many of us forget. By focusing almost exclusively on our physicality, we lose out, dear reader, and many of us pay dearly for this omission. Thankfully, many in the world of physical fitness are beginning to wake up, to shift their underlying philosophy of health. There is a new wave in the fitness world, one that finally recognizes that physical conditioning is only a part of a much larger whole. As Pamela Peek, author of *Fit to Live*, puts it, "It's no longer how big and strong your biceps muscle is, but how big and strong your spiritual and mental muscle is. It's a humanization of fitness into an integrative experience . . . If you want to get anywhere with the body, you start with the mind." This holistic approach recognizes the mind-body as an inseparable unit.

In these pages, I hope to show you a new approach: shifting away from an exclusive focus on weight loss, dieting, and extreme workouts and toward a new regimen of healthful physical wellness. Will you give me this chance? Once again, dear reader, I'm asking you *to change how you think about change*!

In this new approach we come to view the body differently: we recognize and embrace it as an agent and an ally of the program of life changes we seek. If you already work out at the gym because it makes you look better, younger, more attractive—wonderful! What could be better than feeling good about your physical appearance? I salute your hard work and success, dear reader! If you do not, I urge you to consider a moderate program of weight training, flexibility, and cardiovascular exercise—nothing could be physically healthier! But with the Fresh Start program we are after something quite different. We have come here to change our lives. Such a change means using the body to achieve energetic and emotional balance, to give our mind the support it needs to initiate change, to give our mind-body stability as we install, reinforce, and maintain change. In a purely physical workout, we focus on our exterior, on our muscles, tendons, and fibers. In your Fresh Start workout, you will move inward to the body's essential, internal life, to its vibrant and sustaining energies, to the very life force that animates it. When we make this shift, we come to understand the body differently. We learn to balance our essential physical energies, to clear the body of persistent negative energies, to negotiate and rebalance our emotional lives as they are manifested in and through the body. Successful change is about achieving and maintaining balance—any lasting life change is impossible without it. Changing your body's appearance can indeed be wonderful, but it alone will not change the basic conditions of your life. You know this. Becoming happy, satisfied, completely fulfilled, requires deeper body work. It means rising above the powerful unbalancing emotions and negative energies that can undermine desired life change. Anger, frustration, sadness . . . such emotions are a staple of human existence. They cannot be avoided. Yes, they can be temporarily masked by workout endorphins, but as you probably know, they outlast any jogger's high. For successful life change, we learn not to mask or disguise such debilitating emotions, but instead to dissolve them. If we do not, they will reappear. When they do, they will shake and uproot any program of life change. My wonderful news for you: very soon you will start a practical, effective daily program of body-based practices that will finally give you mastery of your emotional and energetic life. Pioneers in the field of mind-body dynamics such as Marjorie Jaffe, author of *The Muscle Memory Method,* have been telling us this for years: when we turn to the inner body and engage it at the deepest level, we harness our most powerful restorative and regenerative agency.

Last week you began to clear the mind of the negative mental patterning that obstructs desired life change. This week you will learn to clear the body of the negative energies and emotions that can sabotage it. With a cleared mind and a cleared body, the life changes you seek become absolutely realizable. Such mastery over your mind-body will bring the victory of life change right to your doorstep.

Will you join me now on this new path?

. . . .

Once upon a time, two young monks were speaking of their Zen masters. The first monk said, "My master is so accomplished he can levitate. In fact, he can even pass through walls!"

"Well, that's a start," responded the second monk.

Astonished, the first monk said, "I'm sure your master cannot do anything more advanced than that!"

The second monk replied, "Actually, he can. My master is so enlightened that he eats when he is hungry and sleeps when he is tired."

. . . .

It is said that there are monks in the Himalayas who dry their monastery linens by draping them over their bodies and, through meditation, raise their body temperatures upward of 110 degrees—they do this, it is said, on high alpine slopes in the middle of winter. Such phenomena fascinate us. Along with passing through matter and levitation, they would make for great party tricks if we could manage them. But here we are after something else. Like the Zen master who learned to eat when hungry and sleep when tired, we want to set our sights on a simpler set of goals—simple goals with profound results. Are you ready to be further transformed? Are you ready for the second stage of your Fresh Start? I hope so! Get ready, then, to forego the extremes of the religion of the body, and to learn, instead, to work *with* and *through* the body to master your physical, energetic, and yes, even your emotional systems.

In the next pages and the next week of your program, you will once again engage in the foundational Fresh Start concepts: *clear* and *create*. You will learn to clear your body of its sluggish, toxic energy and to generate vibrant mind-body energy, which in turn rebalances us physically, mentally, and emotionally. You will transform your view of your body by moving from a Western biochemical orientation to an Eastern energy-based understanding. By doing so, you will learn, perhaps for the first time, to actively and conscientiously love and embrace your body as your self. Along the way, you will also change the way you think about food, sleep, and exercise. You will begin to use the body as a dynamic diagnostic vessel through which you can understand and regulate your physical and mental energy flow. Finally, you will come to fully inhabit your body through the multicolored spectrum of its *chi:* the bioenergetic force that is the basis of life itself. In doing all of this, you will begin to fully master the art of change!

Your discovery of chi will fundamentally change your life: this I can promise you! It will take some time, of course—please remember, change takes practice—but from my years of using such techniques with my clients, I know that your discovery and use of chi's amazing restorative power will prove monumental in your life. You will recognize that you hold within your body the power to cleanse and rejuvenate yourself. This discovery may strike you as a kind of miracle, dear reader, especially if you have been living under the burden of the idea of the "imperfect" body! Come with me now to learn about chi and harness its rebalancing powers. Yes, that's right, by learning this ancient Chinese response to the human narrative, we will engage the body to heal the mind.

Take a deep breath now, loosen that rational Western seatbelt, and prepare to nudge the door of the mind open a bit wider. Do you remember our house metaphor from chapter 1? We are viewing this Fresh Start as a kind of home renovation. We said your conscious awareness resides in the living room of the mind. And you began to refurbish this interior space with new, more vibrant attitudes—loving ones that are conducive to life change. You saw that the space of the mind houses an unconscious library. Here are stored many old volumes and old recordings, many exerting a negative drag upon the self, forestalling change through self-sabotage and judgment. In response, you began to add new volumes and recordings, kind ones that embrace the changes you seek. Finally, and most dramatically, you created a Screening Room. Here, through visualization and self-hypnosis, you began to imagine and thereby create your new future: one based on the life you seek to experience.

I should now like to show you that this house has another essential element, dear reader: a power source that animates it, a kind of electrical system whose energy makes your house a home. It is chi, the fundamental energy of the universe itself!

Have I gone too far this time? Have I stretched your imagination beyond the credible? I hope not, dear friend! I hope that the door of your mind has not suddenly slammed shut! So you ask, and rightly so, what is this chi, and what can it possibly have to do with me and my desire for meaningful life change? I asked this question, too, when I began my journey to life change many years ago. You see, chi was not a word that fell from the lips of my very French grandmother. If there was chi in the south of France where I grew up, somebody had done a pretty good job of hiding it.

WHAT IS CHI?

Like a river throughout our body, chi (pronounced "chee") flows along energetic pathways called *meridians*. You may be at least a little familiar with chi from the practice of acupuncture, which uses needles to catalyze energy movement through these meridians. If it helps, compare chi to the Force in *Star Wars*. Remember when Obi Wan said, "Let the Force be with you"? Good, now you're getting it!

A Short History of Chi

About 3,000 years ago, the ancient art of Chi Gong was born, rooted in the understanding and discovery of chi as the elemental force inhabiting and animating all living things. Chi is seen as two interchangeable forces operative in the universe: yin and yang, the receptive and the ex-pansive. Chi Gong is the practical discipline that grew out of this dis-covery. In Chi Gong, special exercises combine physical conditioning, breathing, and meditation to enhance the circulation of chi. Its object is to regulate internal energy, filling areas of the body that are energy depleted and draining those that are blocked. When chi is properly circulated throughout the body, it flows like mercury, fluid and ani-mate. Soon, and with very little practice, you will feel this movement of energy; you will sense blockages and clear them. When we combine such movement with restorative chi-based breathing, they harmonize to create a self-balancing emotional and energetic system. Your liber-ated chi will gently shift the mind away from preoccupation with daily stress and toward a renewing role. Your body will transform from an emotionally and energetically erratic force, one that can frustrate your life change program, to a harmonizing force that sustains it. You need your body on your side, dear reader! You need to enlist it as an ally of the change you seek.

A Chi Gong master once suggested I think of chi as the spark that ig-nites everything that we do. Let's use our metaphor of the self as a house. Walls, doors, windows, and living quarters do not alone make a habitable space—these themselves are inert. We need an energy system that pow-ers, warms, and lights the space. Only then does it become a home. Chi is this energy, this spark we feel in the sun's rays, the spark that courses through the body, that converts food into energy and strength. We are all born with chi, but just as a house with a flawed electrical system can make life difficult, our own chi supply empties when we do not renew it. Stress is the culprit, and if we are not aware, it will slowly but surely rob us. Under the stress of emotions such as fear, worry, anxiety, and anger, we forego deep, healthy breathing. We develop shallow chest breathing, which provides scant oxygen to the body. Many of us begin to eat junk food and drink multiple cups of coffee in an attempt to re-energize the system, to soothe rising negative emotions. In so doing, we starve our body of its elemental energizing nutrients. Such artificial means only skew the imbalance further. We feel even more sluggish, with very little energy for fully living our lives. We are caught on this merry-go-round of chi depletion. Soon we cannot sustain our life change program because we fall back to our old patterns. Out goes the new, in comes the old. This is not the recipe we are after in our Fresh Start, you will agree!

CHI AND THE PHYSICAL BODY

Here, then, is your new orientation: everything you do, everything you think and eat and listen to and watch, every body function and life activity has a chi result: it either deposits chi into your account (invigorating and rebalancing you) or it makes a chi withdrawal (depleting your energetic system). Soon you will start paying close attention to these habits and behaviors. You will develop an acute awareness of your body's underlying energy. Such awareness will lead you to balance, first in the body and its energetic systems, then in your emotional fields, making us less subject to life's emotional pendulum. Chi-based body balance gives us, ultimately, the harmonious and stable conditions required for lasting change, and that is our goal, is it not?

This practice begins once you start noticing what revitalizes you and what drains you. Chi-mindfulness begins in attention! You will soon see that a program of chi-based movements, some time alone, fresh air, meditations, long walks, belly laughter, lighter and healthier food, sufficient but not excessive sleep . . . all work together to generate new energy; all make chi deposits. You will find yourself engaging in these things more fully and more often. You will begin to develop surplus chi and you will discover the simple joy of chi-awareness, the most elemental human experience. This really is as good as it gets, dear reader!

Hold now in your mind's eye the image of the wolf. Alert, he raises nose, eyes, and ears to every element in his environment, his mind and body in full accord with his deepest being. Such a powerful example of a creature in absolute harmony with itself, its fundamental energies, its world, will serve as a model. You will fashion from this example your new direction, your intention to so raise your awareness of your body energies that you become a fully attuned being. Try now to imagine a wolf skulking through the woods, head bowed by stress, anxiety, and negative thought patterns. Try to imagine the wolf dreading the days ahead. Is it possible? Nonsense. And yet the wolf's life has all the stress imaginable. He must find a mate, feed his young, hunt prey, defend his territory, escape enemies, negotiate the hierarchy of the pack. Such challenges do not deter him. Just the opposite. Such things drive him forward, compel him. In short, they make him the wolf that he is. His life becomes a concerted, harmonized response to these needs, desires, and challenges, fueled by his integrated and magnificently flowing chi. Last week you began to feed the *wolf who would be happy.* This week you will learn to power and restore him. You will be feeding the *wolf who would be powerful!* You will learn how to replace your chi-depleting behaviors with chi-restoring behaviors. As you do this, you will notice the waning of the tendency to complain, to loiter in negativity. You will learn to view your life's challenges and stresses as life-invigorating and life-defining! Working with the body's chi, your mind will follow the body's lead. Your mind will find accordance and integrate itself within the larger mind-body system. Life change will be the result!

CLEAR AND CREATE: YIN AND YANG

What is required to become such a wolf, dear reader, is that we turn again to our foundational Fresh Start concepts, *clear* and *create.* But this week you will clear and create within the framework of the body: you will celebrate a new connection to your body. You will clear the stresses, anxieties, and emotional imbalances that your mind produces but your body experiences. You will create new, positive energy flow, new chi with which to grow, prosper, and master your life changes. Just as you shower and bathe to remove the dirt and bacteria that accumulate on your body daily, so shall you cleanse yourself of your mind-body's negative energies. You will engage in chi-based body practices long known to create new vibrant energy. You will develop an awareness of food as your elemental source of energy (and, sometimes, energy depletion). You will begin to analyze your diet to determine its effects on your chi—you will learn, in turn, corrective dietary measures to help you clear the biochemical agitation caused by chi-depleting eating habits.

As you clear, so shall you create! In clearing and creating, you will give birth to a new body, a new body orientation! In so clearing your body of stagnant chi, you will simultaneously create new chi flow. As the Chinese view it, in yin there is yang—clearing (yin) and creating (yang). So, as far as we are concerned, clearing and creating chi energy are synonymous—they go hand in hand. In so doing, we achieve balance in body and mind, for everything in this new body orientation is circular. Achieving balance means working within an ever-widening circle—using the old to create the new. The breath is the most obvious example. Think of it now, and as you think of it, experience it, for breath is one of your best allies on the path to life change: it is the channel between mind and body, the fundamental mediating force. The in-breath brings oxygen and life, the out-breath expels detritus and waste; the in-breath opens the lungs, the out-breath brings them to a close; the in-breath is the "yes" mechanism, the driving force of creation, the out-breath is the agent of clearance that allows for new life: the completion of the in-breath necessitates the out-breath, and on it goes, each breath distinct, each pairing with the next to generate ongoing life!

In the second week of your Fresh Start program a steady regimen of chi workouts will begin to tone and balance your body from the inside out. Such organic movements will produce many healthful benefits. They help circulate chi, letting the flow of oxygen-rich blood cleanse your body of its toxins. They also massage and cleanse your organs. You will meditate upon your renewed chi flow, your mind will experience the pulse of the primary life force, its warmth will radiate through your body and lead, inevitably, to a sense of comfort and well-being. This is healthful exercise, dear reader! Chi-based therapies generate a kind of human sunshine that lets you grow to heights and dimensions that you have likely never before imagined. When you energize and re-balance yourself to such a degree, you make of yourself a sun to shine on yourself and others, you become a radiant being, transformed and transforming!

Are you ready to begin to fully master these new life arts? Are you ready to shine more luminously? I hope so, dear reader! Shall we then begin the practice of changing the body?

4

The Practice of Changing Your Body

Did chapter 3 open you to a new vision of the body? Did it help you see that the change you seek must also include a new body orientation—one that is affirmative, healthy, joyful? I hope so! Let us go forward now and incorporate the body in our practice of change.

Chapter 4 takes you day by day through the second week of your Fresh Start. Take a moment now to recommit, to resolve to keep finding the time for this—forty minutes a day: twenty in the morning and twenty in the evening. Remember, change takes practice!

Here is your schedule for the second week and the further foundational work that will incorporate your body into your circle of change. Study it. Follow it. This is the path to even greater transformation!

Fresh Start Promise

WEEK TWO DAILY SCHEDULE

DAY 1

Morning
Body-Energy Diagnostic
Discovering Chi: Chi Ball Practice
   (the Accordion of Life)
3Cs Meditation Practice

Evening
Wrist Shake
Sound Therapy: An Introduction
Finger Therapy: An Introduction
Victory Count

DAY 2

Morning
Chi Belly Massage
Morning Breathing Practice
Breath Therapy for Emotional
   Balancing
Fresh Start Question 4

Evening
Arm Swing
Chi Body Massage
Sound Therapy: Second Healing
   Sound
Finger Therapy: Index Finger
Food Seminar

DAY 3

Morning
Chi Belly Massage
Chi Body Massage
3Cs and Screening Room
Five Bites Technique
Mindful Walking

Evening
Arm Swing, Spinal Cord Breathing
Sound Therapy: Third Healing
   Sound
Finger Therapy: Middle Finger
Mindful Eating Practice

DAY 4

Morning
Chi Belly Massage
Morning Breathing Practice
Chi Body Massage
Fresh Start Question 5
Mindful Breakfast Practice
Mindful Warrior Walk

Evening
Arm Swing, Spinal Cord Breathing
Sound Therapy: Fourth Healing
   Sound
Finger Therapy: Ring Finger
Starlit Sky Meditation

DAY 5

Morning
Chi Belly Massage
Morning Breathing Practice
Chi Body Massage
3Cs and Screening Room

Evening
Wrist Shake, Arm Swing, Spinal Cord
  Breathing
Sound Therapy: Fifth Healing Sound
Finger Therapy: Baby Finger
Victory Count

DAY 6

Morning
Chi Belly Massage
Morning Breathing Practice
Fresh Start Question 6
The Lighthouse Meditation

Evening
Wrist Shake, Arm Swing, Spinal Cord
  Breathing
Sound Therapy: Sixth Healing Sound
Finger Therapy Combination
Emergency Release Therapy

DAY 7

Morning
Chi Belly Massage
Morning Breathing Practice
Chi Body Massage
Mindful Eating Practice
Mindful Walking Practice

Evening
Wrist Shake, Arm Swing, Spinal Cord
  Breathing
Sound and Finger Therapy
  Combined
3Cs and Screening Room
Victory Count

Getting Started

This week you'll do your *Fresh Start Promise* activities in two places: in your quiet area and in your bed. Yes, that's right, your bed! Sounds good, doesn't it? About that quiet area: use the same space you used during Week One. This week's healthful exercises, therapies, and rituals build on last week's practices, so the consistency will work for you.

Day №1   Morning

You are in your place? Good. Let's begin. Your three activities for this morning are:

1. Body-Energy Diagnostic

2. Discovering Chi with the "Chi-Ball" Practice

3. 3Cs Meditation Practice

You will start the week by developing awareness of your present physical condition. As you have learned, awareness must precede change. Now you may feel you are already aware; you may already know the answers to the questions below. But I recommend that you write your responses down, if only to confirm this knowledge, and by doing so, to get it into the daylight of the written page. You never know: unexpected answers may also emerge!

Body-Energy Diagnostic

With complete honesty answer the following questions:

A) Emotional Eating Diagnostic   Yes   No

1. When under stress, do you reach for food?   ❏   ❏

2. When under stress, do you lose your appetite?   ❏   ❏

3. Do your food choices sometimes make you feel guilty? ❏   ❏

4. Do you get angry about not being thin?   ❏   ❏

5. Do you actually love your body?   ❏   ❏

6. Do you punish yourself by eating junk food?   ❏   ❏

7. Do you punish yourself *for* eating junk food? ❏ ❏

8. Do you view food as fattening? ❏ ❏

9. Do you struggle with your weight? ❏ ❏

B) Stress Diagnostic   Yes No

1. Do you have a difficult time handling your emotions? ❏ ❏

2. Do you often feel restless? ❏ ❏

3. Do you often feel drained? ❏ ❏

4. Do you have tension headaches? ❏ ❏

5. Does your back ache when you are stressed? ❏ ❏

6. Do you have chronic neck and shoulder tension? ❏ ❏

7. Do you have digestive problems? ❏ ❏

8. Do you experience chest pain and difficulty breathing? ❏ ❏

9. Do you have difficulty falling asleep? ❏ ❏

. . . .

How did you do? Did some of your answers surprise you?

A) Emotional Eating: Five or more "yes" answers. This indicates that you would benefit by fully embracing Week Two's many powerful *Eating Awareness* practices and therapies. Without ignoring or skipping other practices, please give these your absolute attention this week!

B) Stress: Five or more "yes" answers. This means it would be good to fully engage in this week's powerful and enjoyable chi-based practices. These may surprise you with the sense of relaxation and physical and emotional balance they bring.

A) and B): Five or more "yes" answers to both. If this is you, don't despair! For you will enjoy the most dramatic results from this week's wide spectrum of body-based techniques. You are the Fresh Start "chosen people." Your smiles shall be the biggest!

And what about those with a majority of "no" answers in both categories? Well, aren't you wonderful! It's great news that you are doing so well, but if I know your type, I bet you wouldn't mind doing better still! I know that you will still find this week's chi-based program a genuine revelation! Who knows, with more energy you may get even more things done!

Now let's move on to our second activity of the morning.

Discovering Chi:
Chi Ball Practice—the Accordion of Life

This is where it gets exciting, dear friend! No doubt you've had an earful about the link between stress levels and energy levels, but too few people experience directly what good energy, chi energy, actually feels like. This is your moment to discover life's primary force—the dynamic energy Dylan Thomas described in his poem "The Force That Through the Green Fuse Drives the Flower."

Are you ready? Okay, put down your pen and paper and get ready to discover chi through the Chi Ball Practice. I call this Chi Gong exercise the Accordion of Life, and it is the best way for beginners to discover the presence of chi. You don't have to do it every day, but do it at least a few times to get familiar with your primary energy force. After that, use it any time to bring you into the present moment and create relaxation and peace.

1. Rub your hands together for five to ten seconds, until the friction generates some heat.

2. Now move your hands about six inches apart, opening them with fingers spread and rounded. Imagine that you are cradling a solid gold ball in your hands (they should not be touching).

Feel this chi ball and its energy through the activated, tingling sensations in your fingers and palms. Feel its density.

3. Breathe in deeply, and as you do, move your hands farther apart, about two feet. Now move them back in, then out again. Repeat this as if you were playing an accordion. As you play, observe how the ball of energy becomes strings of energy. You might also imagine strings of gold light from the sun.

4. Now, observing even more carefully, notice the sensation of your hands as they are drawn and perhaps even pulled together, as if by the power of two mutually attracting magnets.

5. Continue to inhale and exhale, moving your hands in and out without touching, feeling the energized chi ball expand and contract within your encircling hands. These are yin and yang energies, the primary forces of the universe! This simple exercise demonstrates perfectly balanced energies. Whenever you aim to align and balance the energies of your own body, aim for the same sensation, dear reader.

6. As you continue to open and close your hands, feel your lungs expand and fill with chi. Then feel them contract and expel used, spent chi.

Do at least three rounds, but no more than nine.

The 3Cs Meditation Practice

You should feel peaceful and centered after your Chi Gong exercise. This is an opportune moment to further develop your practice of the 3Cs. With your new sensitivity to chi and your hands-on experience of your body's energetic system, the 3Cs may feel different to you this morning! Pay attention to the body, to the alignment and balance of its primary energies. Today, as you begin to foster this new awareness, you are entering into a new, more integrated relationship with your mind-body, one that will have a profound resonance in your life.

Tip of the Day
ENERGY REBALANCING

What will you do today if you feel tired? Lie down? Sit back or slump lower in your chair? Reach for food, for coffee? Please don't! When you are tired, you *do* need energy, but you need chi energy, not caloric energy, not the replenishing energy of sleep. This may seem counter-intuitive, but the next time you find yourself feeling tired, or overtired, do exactly the opposite of what you think you need to do, of what you used to do. Your prescription is movement, and not slow movement either: quick, vigorous activity is the cure for typical daytime fatigue. You feed your fatigue when you lie down, but when you stand up and mobilize your body you reenergize the system! Treat yourself to a vigorous walk around the block to get that heart going, to revitalize that chi. If you come across a staircase on your walk, wonderful: climb it! If you pass a playground on the way, take a turn on the monkey bars—don't worry, the kids won't mind. Hey, in case you've forgotten, that body of yours was designed to move!

Day №1 Evening

Bonsoir! How was your day?

Did you get out your chi ball? Did you experience body awareness at least a few times today? You were more aware of the sensation of stress, perhaps? That may not seem like the greatest advance, I agree! That's okay, because tonight you will learn to clear such stress and make room for more joyful body experiences. Are you ready to learn? Good. Here's what you will do:

1. Evening Cleansing Rituals: Wrist Shake

2. Sound Therapy: Introduction and First Healing Sound

3. Finger Therapy: Introduction and Thumb Grab

4. Victory Count

Evening Cleansing Rituals

I would like now to introduce you to some simple body-cleansing rituals: yes, rituals. They are positively charged rituals—not neutral exercises—because they signal to your mind-body that you are worthy of feeling better and that you are willing to do the work needed. These concrete daily actions will become sacred and precious to you, dear reader. These are simple but profoundly transformative acts of loving kindness to yourself—rituals enacted in observance of your right, your need to feel better, to feel good. Soon life will be unimaginable without them! So let's begin.

WRIST SHAKE

Stand up. Now shake your wrists vigorously nine times clockwise and nine times counterclockwise. As body extremities, your wrists accumulate tension. By moving them, you will begin to move stress and anxiety out of the body, where they are stored, and into the world, where they belong. The number of repetitions is important: nine is the last of the single-digit numbers and, in the Chinese system, stands for completion and contentment. Allow for some mystery in your life by observing this convention, even if you don't yet understand it!

Have you done your wrist shake? Good. Now please stay standing. Place your feet shoulder-width apart, planting them firmly. Now, with your arms hanging by your sides like wet Chinese noodles, shake your entire body up and down. As you do so, visualize that you are *shaking off and away* gray, sluggish energy, stagnant chi. Do this for at least a minute. Then stand perfectly still and do the 3Cs meditation. Yes, that's right—these are the vertical Cs. Deepen your body awareness by simply feeling the sensations that emanate. Having completed the 3Cs, place both your hands over your navel and smile the inner smile of contentment. Savor the absence of negative energies in the body and embrace the sensations of active chi, your primary life force!

Sound Therapy: An Introduction

Now you can sit! Find a comfortable chair and get ready to do something weird! This practice might seem odd at first, but it brings amazing results. You are about to make some strange but liberating noises!

One principle of traditional Chinese medicine is that each body organ is linked with an emotion. By uttering the specific sound associated with each organ, you will liberate that emotion and, in the process, restore mind-body balance. There are six of these sounds, each linked to an organ: lungs, kidneys, liver, heart, gallbladder, and "triple warmer." What's that, you ask? Not exactly an organ, the triple warmer is an important energy meridian associated with digestion and the emotive qualities of discernment and acceptance.

Tonight we will start with the first sound: SSSSS, like a serpent hissing. It releases anxiety—and that will bring you courage. You will repeat the SSSSS sound five times. Try it now for practice. Sit with your feet flat on the floor. Take a deep breath in for four counts. As you exhale, hiss—SSSSS—for as long as you can, ideally for the count of eight. Repeat five times. At the end of each cycle, take a minute to meditate on the emotion of courage and silently repeat the words *I can, I do, I will.* Invite courage and strength into your life. Foster gratitude for this experience; smile and thank your lungs for breathing life into your body.

How did you do? Did you feel a release in your mind-body?

Let us now move to one more body practice for tonight's session. This may strike you as another strange way to bring about change, but keep the door of the mind open, dear reader!

Finger Therapy: An Introduction

This practice is based on a Japanese energy discipline called Jin Shin Jitsu, an ancient tradition similar to Chinese acupuncture. It is based on the idea that each of our five fingers (including the thumb) is linked to an emotion. By holding the finger for a minute, or for the time you need to experience your pulse, you will regain mind-body balance.

To remember which is which, think of *worry fast.* The thumb is W for *worry,* the index finger is F for *fear,* the middle finger is A for *anger* (as one might expect), the ring finger is S for *sadness,* and the little finger it T for *trying hard.*

Tonight we shall begin with the thumb. Sitting quietly, breathing deeply and slowly, gently wrap your left thumb with the fingers of your right hand. Hold it for a minute or so, until you feel a pulsing sensation—and as you do so, imagine all your worries melting away. Smile at this experience! Accept it with appreciation.

Victory Count

REFLECT ON YOUR DAY IN A POSITIVE WAY

Do one more thing tonight: write down three victories of the day, no matter how small. Acknowledge them as successes. Give yourself credit. Be grateful!

. . . .

So that's about it for tonight. I hope you have enjoyed these simple but valuable rituals of your first night of body-based practices. These exercises might seem peculiar, perhaps strange, perhaps even unsubstantial, but I ask that you trust that they are practical means of working with your body to clear its negative stresses and emotions.

Day № 2   Morning

Good morning! Today you will treat yourself to a massage, then start to learn some other practices which, like showering and brushing your teeth, will become essential morning rituals. You will build on them throughout Week Two. Let's start with this morning's activities:

1. Chi Belly Massage
2. Morning Breathing Practice
3. Breath Therapy for Emotional Balancing
4. Fresh Start Question 4

First, your massage. Are you out of bed? If so, that's okay. You have two options: either go back to bed or, if that's too risky, head for the couch. Starting tomorrow, however, you will do these self-massages in the sanctuary of your own bed, soon after waking. They only take a minute or so, but they will make an enormous difference in how you and your body face the day.

Chi Belly Massage

This massage is an essential chi diagnostic. Circling your abdomen, you will press gently at two-inch intervals, feeling for sore spots that indicate a blockage of chi energy. Once you have found them, you will gently massage them until your chi flows freely once again.

Place the fingers of both hands on your solar plexus: the "pit of the stomach" just below the base of the sternum. Press down deeply and exhale. Now slowly move your hands about two inches to the right, press down again and exhale—this is the area of your pancreas. Move another two inches to the right—again, press down and exhale—this is your liver area. Continue in a circle around the abdomen, pressing down every two inches and exhaling. The massaged area is a band about six inches wide, extending from just below the sternum to an inch or two below the navel. As you continue along your way, you will be examining and massaging your small intestine, colon, gallbladder, and stomach. After making a complete counterclockwise circle, finish off with quick, circular belly rubs: nine clockwise, nine counterclockwise. This will get that essential chi force flowing in what the Chinese call *Dan Tiem,* your body's power center, its center of gravity.

Then place your hands flat against your navel: right hand underneath for women, left hand underneath for men. Would you like to know why? Because women are right! Voilà—that is the answer my Chi Gong master gave me, and I love it! Holding your hands here, stay still for the following breathing practice.

Morning Breathing Practice

This is a powerful means of reconnecting mind to body and improving concentration.

Begin by fixing your awareness on the top of your head, feeling for its actual physical sensation. While doing so, breathe *in* and up to this spot, following the sensation of your breath as it enters your lungs, rises up your neck, and arrives at the top of your head. When you exhale, breathe *down* from the head, expelling the breath down through the body. Repeat this action, doing your best to focus on the palpable sensation of breath energy as you draw it up through the body to the head, and down to the toes. This might take some practice!

Now repeat this action, only this time count each inhale-exhale cycle, saying "one" as you breathe in to the top of your head and out to the toes, "two" on the next in-breath, and so on. Complete nine breath cycles. See if you can keep your mind focused solely on sensation—it will likely stray to other thoughts, to the concerns that so often preoccupy it. That's okay; when you notice that your mind has moved off topic, gently bring it back to sensation. Cultivate an accepting attitude toward your constantly straying mind, my friend! The Buddhists call the untrained mind a "monkey mind" for its tendency to distract itself by constantly picking things up, examining them, turning them over, jumping to the next thing, and the next, and the next. By learning to concentrate the mind, you will develop much higher awareness. It also helps keep you in the present moment, the only reality there can possibly be.

As you may remember, yesterday we began to develop a new awareness of stress's effects on our bodies, moods, and, very importantly, eating habits. Today we will consider some practical wisdom on the links between stress, emotions, and food cravings.

Breath Therapy for Emotional Balancing

As a result of events and crises in our daily lives, we may often be unbalanced by strong emotions. Such unbalancing can lead to emotional eating and other habits from which we now seek liberation. In the following exercises, breath is the means of returning the self to balance, to the present moment. These are simple but powerful techniques for maintaining equilibrium in the face of life's challenges.

1. **When Overwhelmed by Anger.** Focus your awareness and your intention on your breath; cultivate long, deep exhalations through the mouth; visualize anger and frustration being channeled and cleansed from the body through the vehicle of the breath.

2. **When Feeling a Strong Need for Nurture and Love.** Focus your awareness and your intention on your breath; cultivate long, deep inhalations through your nose; visualize nurturing, life-giving oxygen being drawn into the heart.

3. **When Feeling Unbalanced or "Spacy."** Focus your awareness and your intention on your breath; cultivate long, soft, rhythmic inhalations and exhalations through your nose; visualize the anchoring,

life-sustaining agency of oxygen being drawn into the lungs, and the mind-body's agitations being expelled from lungs into the air.

Let's now move on to the first body-based diagnostic question of week two.

Fresh Start Question 4

Reflect on this question before answering: be honest and be specific.

What is draining your energy?

What is the most common drain on your essential energy, your life force, your chi? Is it overwhelming emotion? Which emotion? Is it anger, or anxiety, or a feeling of helplessness? Is it stress? What is the source? Whatever it is, commit your answer to paper and keep it in your mind throughout your day, in particular when you are feeling drained. Begin to establish connections between this sensation and the emotional or external events that trigger it. Increase your awareness of the causality at work here, dear reader: this is the key to overcoming it. Acknowledge the cause or causes of this drain on your energetic system and develop and express self-compassion when you find yourself in this depleted state. Immediately turn to the breathing practices or any of this chapter's other techniques that you have found helpful. Practice these techniques as an act of compassion to yourself and with the knowledge that not only will they bring relief, over time they will also begin to get at the root causes of these emotions and eventually dissipate them. This takes time, so be patient—remember, change begins in awareness—life change is developed through concrete, specific, responsive actions. Taking action to bring relief will in itself bring comfort, calm, and balance (helplessness increases emotional imbalance, but directed, loving actions restore equilibrium).

As you travel, consciously plan and intend to have a great day. Make this a daily mission: meditate on the fact that you are no longer helpless in the face of unbalancing emotions—you are now armed with practical techniques for rebalancing, for creating those great days you desire and deserve! Go gentle and love yourself when things go awry. You need not simply suffer through such events, you can now take positive and concrete actions to calm and heal yourself! Take care, my friend! The best of all possible days to you! See you tonight!

Tip of the Day
SLOW DOWN

What will you do if you feel hyper or tense today? Will you speed your pace, run around, try to get more things done, try to burn off all that energy? Think again! Here's the chi-based cure for overabundant energy: slow down! You've got energy and that feels good, right? Much better than fatigue, anyway. But you may be feeling an overabundance of nervous, anxious energy. This isn't the kind you want to have; this is chi-depleting energy. Over time, it will use up and deplete the body of its essential core energies and resources. So once again, do the opposite of what you usually do, of what you think you need to do. Slow it down considerably! Observe the breath, do a meditation. Sit down. Relax. That's it, you've got it now!

Day №2   Evening

How did your day go? Did you remember to use the techniques you have been practicing to create the kind of day you desire? Did you have cravings, and, importantly, did you use your breathing exercises as a constructive and healing response to them?

Tonight you will build your ability to physically release and clear accumulated body stress. Sounds good, doesn't it? Hold off on the wine or the martini and give these rituals a try! Here's what you will do:

1. Evening Cleansing Rituals: Arm Swing

2. Chi Body Massage

3. Sound Therapy: Second Healing Sound

4. Finger Therapy: Index Finger Grab

5. Fresh Start Food Seminar

Evening Cleansing Rituals

ARM SWING

Stand up. Are you vertical? Good. Now free your arms by allowing them to hang loosely at your sides. Okay, now swing them way up from your sides, raising them outstretched above your head. As you do so, push your hips forward. Then, release your arms back down to your sides, to their original position. Now repeat, using this visualization: you are on a swing, a very long swing. Feel the freedom of your arms as they swing freely upward and past your head. As you release your arms from their raised position, feel and visualize their free return to your sides.

Repeat this ritual nine times.

Then stand perfectly still. Concentrate on your fully liberated arms, which now hang freely. Now move your awareness from your arms to the top of your head. From the crown of your head, a golden beam ris-es, an energized force that pulls you gently skyward into the realm of infinite possibilities. Once you have this sensation, add to it the coun-terbalancing awareness of your feet firmly rooted to the floor, to the nurturing earth. Be present to these dual, complementary sensations: your head raised toward infinite space and possibility, your legs and feet rooted to the grounding earth. Focus your awareness on the pro-found and elemental balance between these two realms. Be with this moment, hold yourself firmly within this balance of body connected to the heavens, feet connected to the earth.

Use this sensation to build on your knowledge of yin-yang balance.

Chi Body Massage

This terrific set of exercises re-energizes both mind and body (and thus spirit!). It will actually be part of your morning routine, but it can be done anytime, anywhere (although if you do it in a public space, be pre-pared to attract attention). You can stand up or sit down, do the whole set or only selected parts. As you do it, evaluate how each exercise reju-venates your mind and body—some will work more powerfully than others. And, dear reader, though many of these techniques may seem odd or even silly, trust for now that each is a fully legitimate part of the ancient Chinese practice of Chi Gong, the art of regulating and enhanc-ing the flow of life's primal force. Soon you will experience their value for yourself. Soon, instead of reaching for caffeine, you will find yourself reaching for your ears, your forehead, the back of your neck.

Note: In Chi Body Massage, contact between your hand and specif-ically targeted body areas will stimulate your chi flow. Don't be afraid to use vigor where appropriate!

1. Using stiff fingers, vigorously tap your skull all over, temples, lobes, everywhere! This is an excellent way to energize your chi and your blood flow. It will also awaken sleeping or dormant brain cells—no kidding!

2. Now gently tap the forehead only—an amazing way to clear emotion-based stresses.

3. Gently tap your face—yes, that's right, your precious face! In addition to its invigorating effects, this is also a natural facelift. It will keep your skin supple and smooth by ensuring movement of essential moisture and oils.

4. Pull your ears. Go ahead, give them a good tug, they won't fall off. (If they do, let me know and I'll refund the price of the book!. This is an effective way to maintain mental alertness—excellent for those long afternoons in the office, or those dreaded meetings. It also works well at the opera.

5. Using both index fingers, brush behind your ears. This will revitalize your liver and help detoxify your body.

6. Brush the back of your neck with both hands, from top to bottom. This relieves tension.

7. Brush your throat from top to bottom, alternating hands. This stimulates your thyroid and regulates metabolism.

8. Knead your shoulders to unburden yourself of muscle- and cell-stored tension.

9. Tap your sternum (centered between your ribs, about two inches below your collarbone). This technique is greatly enhanced by humming—seriously! Hum as you tap, and experience the benefits of improved thymus function. Often called the "anti-cancer gland," the thymus is a crucial element of your immune system.

10. Making two fists, vigorously pound your lungs like Tarzan. If your relationship with your neighbors allows, make the Tarzan sound: UUHHHH, OOUUOOHHH, UUHHHH.

11. Slap your legs vigorously all over, front and back. This is good for circulation and strengthens your bones.

12. Lean forward, bring your chest down to waist level, reach behind you, make fists and drum on your lower back. This helps
relax the muscles.

13. Finally, stand up (if you haven't already) and give yourself a
good shaking. That's right, shake! Shake the body out. This
is a great way to complete your Chi Body Massage and fully
activate all your energetic meridians.

I hope you enjoy these exercises, but enjoyment aside, this practice
will have an amazingly positive effect on your energetic system. Don't
let their simplicity and ease fool you; their effects are not superficial.
These are ancient, time-tested ways to manage chi, to clear away stagnant energies, to create new, positively charged ones. Such techniques
move you away from being a passive victim, toward becoming an active
director of your body's energy system. Which would you rather be?

Let's now move on to the healing and rebalancing power of Sound
Therapy, which you first engaged in last night and which you will
practice every night of your second Fresh Start week.

Sound Therapy: Second Healing Sound

For tonight's sound, form the mouth into the shape it makes when
blowing out a candle. Then you'll blow it out! That's what this sound is:
the sound and action of blowing out a candle. Its therapeutic function
is to release fears and replace them with what can best be called trust
and faith. Repeat the candle sound five times. As usual, breathe in for
four counts, out for eight. After completing the sound, take three slow,
deep breaths and declare, "I am willing to trust. I let go of my fears. I
have faith in the goodness of the universe." Finish up by generating the
inner smile of contentment and directing that positive energy toward
your kidneys (in the area of your back directly opposite your navel).

Finger Therapy: Index Finger Grab

Sitting quietly, breathing deeply and slowly, gently wrap your left index finger with the fingers of your right hand. Hold your index finger for about a minute, until you feel a pulsing sensation. As you do so, imagine all of your fears melting away. Smile at this experience! Accept it with appreciation and gratitude.

I hope you are feeling considerably more peaceful and balanced after completing tonight's Fresh Start evening rituals. Take a moment to enjoy this peace and to recognize how deserving you are of its healthful and life-affirming benefits. Promise yourself a regular diet of such joy, such contentment. As you proceed on your path, may you enjoy many more such moments of tranquility.

Before we finish tonight, let's turn to the subject of food and reconsider its value and role in your life—and in your quest to become happier.

Fresh Start Food Seminar

As you move ahead with your Fresh Start program, you are becoming more highly attuned to your body's physical needs for energy, emotional balance, and the release of accumulated stresses and anxieties. Wonderful!

In these first two weeks, you are also growing more understanding, more loving toward your entire being, your entire self. Now is the time to join these two new positive attitudes (sensitivity to bodily needs, and compassion toward self) to address the important subject of food: what you eat and how you eat it.

Dear reader, now is the time to cultivate in yourself the faith that you will, from this day forward, begin to eat food that is nourishing for your body, in quantities that are suitable to its needs. Now is the time to choose to eat, and trust that you will continue to eat, food that will make you vibrant, strong, alert, and, above all, happy. It is also a great time to jettison the baggage that accompanies food: the guilt, the tendency toward self-deprivation and the resulting overindulgence—and begin to abandon these and other negative attitudes and anxieties regarding food. Trust that from now on you will place your faith in your desire to be healthy and fit and thinner, especially if these make up one of your primary goals. Begin to express your intentions positively: "I choose to be healthy" instead of "I need to lose weight." These new affirmative attitudes have been rising from your subconscious as a result of your work in the screening room, but you should now also be maintaining them in your living room, your room of conscious awareness.

Sometimes you will eat crazy things. Life is, after all, meant to be lived, not meant to be a protracted exercise in self-deprivation, in saying "no." But with your growing sensitivity to actual body needs, you will find yourself moderating such indulgences. This will not be a matter of willpower or denial, but of loving awareness of your actual needs. You don't have to deprive yourself of what you want if what you want is to be healthy.

From now on, then, when you have the urge to eat, check in with yourself to make sure your body actually needs to eat. If you have eaten recently, if your body isn't in actual need of caloric energy, stay for a moment in this awareness. Take a deep, calming breath and ask yourself what you actually need at this moment. Frame the question positively—How do I want to feel? What do I actually need?—rather than asking, What do I feel like eating? What do I want to eat?

By posing these questions, you will begin to clarify your needs, clarify your intentions. If you are hungry, you will, of course, eat and enjoy the act of eating. But surprisingly often you will find emotional needs behind your desire for food. You will find other, more appropriate, more loving actions you can take to satisfy such emotional needs—this chapter is full of them!

Eating with awareness, eating more slowly and deliberately (by chewing consciously, for example), posing questions about your actual needs—all these practices promote a new orientation, a new conditioning regarding food and diet. If you find it useful, you may choose to view them as a kind of self-governing weight-watching program that does not rely on others: no support group needed. Foster trust, faith, and confidence in your own abilities to successfully manage your eating life!

So from now on before you eat, clarify your intentions and diagnose your actual physical needs. Are they physical or emotional? Are you eating to optimize your health, because your cells need nourishment? Or are you indulging yourself? If the latter, fine, treat yourself to something special, but be aware that this is what you are doing, that you are eating for reward!

Finally, before you eat, consider how you want to feel *after* eating. Do you want to feel alert, focused, and energized? Wonderful! Keep these goals in mind when making your food selections. You may want, on the other hand, to relax, to feel sleepy. If this is your desire, choose accordingly. Healthy eating begins and ends in body awareness.

If you were expecting me to take a rigid, unforgiving attitude toward food, you can relax now. I am French, remember! I love food and I love to eat well. I do not believe that life should consist of an endless round of small, dutiful portions of raw foods, nuts, and soybeans. But nor do I believe it should be an endless smorgasbord. Eating well, eating healthy is about balance. It's about eating with intention, it's about finding joy and *joie de vivre* in the simplest and humblest of meals.

Basic Food Awareness

Now that we have established clarity and intention as the cornerstones of healthful eating practices, let's close off the evening with some essential information about food and its effects on the body. You may already be familiar with this material—if so, by all means, skip it and we'll say good night and see you in the morning. If you're not sure, read on—this could be very helpful to you in making the right food choices. However, it does not take the place of professional advice. See a qualified nutritionist or doctor to address your own needs.

YOU AND YOUR BLOOD SUGAR

You need a small amount of glucose circulating in your blood to fuel your body's metabolic processes. Since your body is finely attuned to the presence of glucose, it's best to try to keep your blood sugar levels steady. If you eat a lot of carbohydrates or sweets, your blood sugar will first spike and then crash, which can cause mood swings and other negative symptoms. Avoid such spikes and crashes, since they don't do much to promote overall balance!

As much as possible, choose, instead, foods from the low end of the glycemic spectrum. Also known as the "low carbs," such staples as vegetables, beans, and legumes will help control your appetite, reduce mood swings, enhance alertness, and keep your body balanced.

EATING FOR ACID/ALKALINE BALANCE

When the blood is too acidic, the body pulls calcium from the bones to neutralize the acid. This causes osteoporosis, and, some believe, is the basis for almost all disease. In his book *The pH Miracle,* nutritional theorist Dr. Robert Young describes this excess acid: "If left unchecked it will interrupt all cellular activities and functions from the beating of your heart to the neuro-firing of your brain. Over-acidification interferes with life itself . . . all regulatory systems, including breathing, circulation, digestion, [and] hormone production become exhausted."

To avoid such imbalance, eat alkalizing foods; these include most fruits, vegetables, and seeds. Reduce your intake of acidic foods such as animal proteins.

EATING FOR ENERGY: YOUR MINI-GUIDE

- Eat vegetables, whole grains, legumes, nuts, and fruit. Fish is a healthy source of protein.

- Eat several small meals and snacks every day instead of a huge meal or meals. Eat something every four to six hours during the day— this will help you maintain steady energy.

- Reduce your wheat intake. Wheat can make you feel bloated and sluggish.

- Choose alkalizing foods. The optimum ratio for most people is 75 percent alkalizing foods to 25 percent acidifying foods.

- Minimize your sugar intake—and not only white sugar. Watch out for all white foods, including refined sugar, potatoes, white flour, and dairy products. Sugar lurks in unexpected places! If you decide to indulge in a protein bar, choose a low-carbohydrate one.

- Drink herbal teas between meals to flush out your body toxins.

- Chew well! Digestion begins in the mouth.

- Healthy snacks include almonds, guacamole, edamame (prepared soybeans), fresh or frozen steamed vegetables (keep leftover steamed squash, broccoli, and cauliflower in your refrigerator).

- Choose olive oil and eat flax seeds to boost your Omega 3 fatty acids: especially important for women's hormonal balance.

- Eat an apple every day. An apple a day keeps the doctor away—this is actually true, imagine that!

- When eating dessert, take two bites and enjoy them fully. On the third bite, ask yourself, "Do I want to take another bite that will taste exactly like the last two?"

- Instead of a cappuccino, drink green tea.

Day №3   Morning

Bonjour! Welcome to Day Three. I hope you enjoyed yesterday's morning rituals. Remember, it is best to do these body exercises from the warmth and sanctuary of your bed in the moments after waking—this will help you reconnect your head to your body! In all, here are this morning's activities:

1. Chi Belly Massage

2. Chi Body Massage

3. 3Cs and Screening Room Practice

4. Five Bites Technique for Mindful Eating

5. Mindful Walking Practice

Chi Belly Massage

I would like you to initiate your morning rituals with the Chi Belly Massage you learned yesterday. As you begin your practice, try to put that smile of contentment on your face, and direct gratitude to your heart for the gift of your life in this world. Recognize your loving commitment to yourself and your program of change. Lastly, affirm your desire and intention to have a positive and joyful day!

Have you finished your belly massage? Excellent! Now sit up on the edge of the bed and bring out your chi ball. If you have forgotten where it is, please refer back to Day One's morning instructions.

Chi Body Massage

Now that you have energized your hands with positive chi energy, begin your massage. Again, if you have forgotten the particulars, please refer to Day Two's evening instructions.

The 3Cs and Screening Room Practice

Now, while you are still on the edge of your bed, sensitive to your innate chi energy, finish off your bed rituals with the 3Cs practice, followed by the Screening Room. Now that you are in your second week, you should be comfortable with these two foundational Fresh Start exercises. Coming after the grounding, reconnective body rituals, these two mind-based practices should help you manifest greater mental clarity, thus reinforcing your desired visions of change. Such a combination is also an amazing way to prepare yourself for a great day!

Five Bites Technique for Mindful Eating

This morning I would like to share with you a secret that has changed many of my clients' waistlines, helping them to forever transform their approach and attitude to food, body, and self.

Let me illustrate this technique with a client story. Katherine was a very successful young attorney. She worked many long hours in the office preparing cases. Naturally, she always ended up eating on the run, and eating too much of the wrong food. She was frequently beset by intensive sugar cravings that she found difficult to resist. As a result of these lifestyle and eating habits, Katherine weighed twenty pounds more than she wanted to, was unhappy with her appearance, yet resisted the idea of a strict diet because food was her primary source of comfort: it gave her joy and much-needed relief from stress.

I told Katherine that she could continue to eat anything she wanted on one condition: that after the fifth bite of every meal, she would put down her fork, lean back in her chair, take three deep breaths, and visualize each breath filling her with peace, freedom, and relaxation. After this breathing ritual, she could continue to eat, but only after answering two food awareness questions: (1) *Am I actually tasting what I am eating?* and (2) *Won't the next bite taste exactly like the previous bite?*

Katherine was to let her answers determine her course of action: would she (a) finish *all* the food on her plate, (b) finish *some* of the food on the plate, or (c) *leave* the food on her plate because she had satisfied her body's need for nourishment and her mind's desire for comfort and joy?

After a week of the five bites practice, Katherine called me in a state of shock. Not only had she already lost three pounds without paying any attention to her diet, she had also, for the first time in her life, begun to leave food on her plate. To Katherine, this was a miracle! She was in control of her eating for the first time ever. Not only that, mealtimes now brought her emotional equilibrium, a sense that she was in charge. Gone were feelings of shame and self-judgment. This simple practice brought substantive changes to both her body and her self-worth. Try this today at lunch, dear reader. This practice, so helpful, so positive in its results, may bring you such a miracle as well!

Mindful Walking Practice

I will leave you with one final exercise, my friend. I will describe it for you now, but you will not actually practice it until after you head out the door on your way to your day. You can practice it throughout your day, however.

Walking mindfully is a practice that originates in the East. It is used as a form of meditation, one that helps establish awareness, or mindfulness, as it is more accurately called.

I first witnessed this on a visit to Thailand. I was spending the day at a Buddhist temple, meditating and exploring the grounds and surrounding countryside. That afternoon, I spotted a monk, bald-headed, saffron-robed, walking through the gardens, but walking in a way I had never before witnessed, a way I would never forget: he was moving slowly, fully concentrated, fully engaged in the simple act of walking. Simply by placing one foot in front of the other, he seemed to be at absolute peace with himself and his environment. He was serene. He seemed filled with reverence. All I could do was watch amazed as this monk made his way through the gardens in a state of absolute awareness and grace.

About a year later I had the very good fortune to attend a talk by Thich Nhat Hanh, the Buddhist master, teacher, and poet, and I learned more about what I had witnessed that day at the temple garden. Explaining the mindfulness walking technique that had so entranced me, Thich Nhat Hanh provided the following instruction: "When you walk, think that you are kissing the earth with your feet and that you are touching the sky with your eyes." What an exquisite metaphor! What a perfect description of what I had seen that day.

One does not have to be a monk to walk like this! On your way to work, or at lunch today, carry with you Thich Nhat Hanh's evocative instruction: become aware of your feet making contact with the earth. Feel the sensation as your foot touches down. Notice how your other leg and foot come naturally forward. Note the interval when this leg and foot are suspended in air, then bring your awareness to its touching down upon the world. On your next set of steps, imagine that your feet are connecting you to the earth, that your eyes connect you to the heavens. Balance and experience these complimentary, harmonizing sensations: foot *kissing* the earth, head *connecting* to the heavens. Once you have this awareness, complement it with deep, slow, grateful breaths of golden, chi-filled air. And if you can, complete your mindful walk with a smile of satisfaction at being this very person in this very place. I wish you much joy and contentment in your day, dear reader! May you arrive at the destination *you* choose.

Day №3   Evening

Bonsoir! How did your day go? I hope you did some meditative walking on your lunch, or on the way home. Did you practice the five bites technique? How much food did you eat after answering those questions? I hope you were honest!

Let's begin now with some healthful practices to unwind the accumulated tensions of the day and arrive at a calm and contented place! This evening's activities:

1. Evening Cleansing Rituals: Arm Swing, Spinal Cord Breathing

2. Sound Therapy: Third Healing Sound

3. Finger Therapy: Middle Finger Grab

4. Mindful Eating Practice

Evening Cleansing Rituals

ARM SWING

You've done this one before. Once again, begin by swinging your arms out and upward until they are well above your head. As you do so, imagine yourself free of gravity, sailing through the air on a great swing. This time, as your arms are just about to return to their starting position, give out a great, audible sigh of relief—understanding, as you do so, that by swinging your arms in this way, you are dissolving the tensions that have accumulated in your body's cells and tissues throughout the day. Promote this clearance by visualizing these unwanted tensions as they leave your body through the medium of your outstretched swinging arms and fingers. Send this unwanted energy back into the world!

When you have done nine rounds of arm swinging, stop. Let your liberated arms come to rest at your sides. Be perfectly still for at least a moment or two. Observe the sensations in your arms and upper body. Do you feel the tingle and dance of the new, vibrant energies that arose once you made room for them? Be with this healthful energy for just a moment longer. Is this how you would like to feel?

Let's follow up with a practice that is highly recommended for aching backs, but, importantly, it also replenishes kidney energy. Often, by the end of day, this energy has been considerably diminished by adrenal depletion, a side effect of protracted stress.

SPINAL CORD BREATHING

Okay, stand with your feet shoulder-width apart, arms at your sides. Make two fists. Now the best way to learn this is to run through it in slow motion a couple of times to make sure you are coordinating properly. First, from the trunk, twist your upper body slowly to the right. As you reach the limit of your twist, bring your left fist across the front of your body to strike your right shoulder, while simultaneously bringing your right fist behind the back of your body to strike your lower back. Now repeat in the opposite direction. Twist left with your right fist contacting your left shoulder, left fist contacting your lower back. Once you're comfortable in the practice, do five rounds, adding the strong karate sound to each fist-to-body contact: HA! Let the HA come from deep in the belly, not from the shallowness of the throat. A sound originating in the throat feels and sounds weak, almost hesitant; a sound generated in the belly, your place of power, sounds strong, decisive, resonant. Such a vocalization is the perfect complement to this exercise. Experience your power and your resilience as you pound shoulders and back—you are strong, you are a warrior!

Express gratitude for this moment.

Sound Therapy: Third Healing Sound

Tonight we move on to SHHHH, the third healing sound, the sound for the liver. SHHHH helps dissipate the energy of anger, replacing it with the energy of patience and kindness. Remember your in-breath (to the count of four). On the out-breath, make the SHHHH sound, ideally for the count of eight. Do this five times, meditating upon the emotion of kindness, especially kindness toward your self. Imagine substituting the warm goodness of this feeling for the acidic heat of anger. Finish by sending the warmth of that kindness smilingly down your body to the liver, thanking it for its function in cleansing your body of impurities and helping you be a healthy being.

A final note: the next time you find yourself starting to use another word that begins with a SH sound, likely in expression of anger or frustration, remember that you have in your tool kit a different SH sound that converts anger to kindness!

Let's now move from the therapeutic power of sound to the healing power of touch in our bid to dissolve anger and other strong negative emotions within the body.

Finger Therapy: Middle Finger Grab

Not surprisingly, the middle finger represents and embodies annoyance, frustration, and anger. Gently wrap the middle finger of your left hand with the fingers of your right hand. Hold this position until you feel a pulsing sensation. Once you have this, imagine and visualize all your anger and frustration melting away, becoming absorbed by the middle finger. Hold this image and any accompanying sensation for at least a minute. Know that you have contained all your mind-body's anger within your middle finger—you may be tempted to use it, to give it away to the first person who crosses you, but don't! Such an act will release your contained anger, allowing it to run through your body again, creating even more misery. Keep your anger in your finger and let it slowly, naturally dissipate. Smile at this thought. Enjoy this moment!

Mindful Eating Practice

Let's close this evening's Fresh Start rituals with a delicious and compelling little exercise in mindful eating. You will need a dried cranberry or raisin, or a fresh grape, for this exercise. If you don't have any of these, buy some tomorrow and practice this exercise tomorrow night.

This is an unforgettable experience that has the power to transform your approach to food forever, my friend. I have shared this practice with many clients who suffer from emotional eating issues. When I hand them a cranberry or a grape, they invariably laugh, wondering whatever it is that a minuscule piece of fruit could possibly do to help them with their eating. Of course, this is precisely the point.

Here's your instruction:

1. Place a single cranberry (or other fruit) inside your palm.

2. Take some time to look at it, to notice its smallness, the color of its skin, its texture and shape, the way the light reflects off it.

3. Slowly and mindfully, bring it to your lips. Bring your full awareness to its touch, its texture against your lips.

4. Here comes the crucial moment. Ever so slowly, place it in your mouth. Note the location and lightness of this tiny piece of fruit on your tongue.

5. Now focus on your desire to bring your teeth down upon it, to bite into it, to eat it. Don't do any of these things just yet, just be absolutely aware of these sensations, these desires.

6. Take some deep breaths as you continue to observe these sensations without acting or reacting to them. Sit back. Relax!

7. Okay, now prepare to act, to do the thing that your mind-body so wants you to do: place the cranberry between your teeth. Hold it there a moment, then slowly, mindfully, bite into it. As you do so, notice keenly the explosion of flavors, the tangy sweetness of the fruit.

8. Now slowly chew it until the fruit is fully dissolved. Swallow it and concentrate on the aftertaste lingering on your tongue.

Voilà! Victory to you, dear reader! How did you do? Was this an agonizing experience? Or was it blissful? Did you find it frustrating? Did you want to speed up the process, break into the berry, chew it, swallow it? Did it drive you absolutely nuts?

For most people, this experience leads to the knowledge that when they eat normally, they rarely take the time to fully savor their food. Imagine, for a moment, eating this way always. Imagine eating slowly, mindfully, enjoying the multi-layered sensations of food's textures, colors, smells, and flavors.

Imagine the positive implications of such a mindful eating practice. Such eating would greatly magnify the pleasures of food. Such eating would lead you to eat less and enjoy more. I can't make you begin to eat this way, of course; only you can do this. For now, just remember that you *can* slow down, you *can* enjoy your food more. In so doing, you can enjoy the benefits of eating less while giving nothing up in return—just the opposite, as you have learned. Consider this experience in the days and meals that follow. Change begins in awareness! In dreams begin responsibilities.

Used together, the Five Bites and Mindful Eating practices can transform both your eating experience and your waistline—an unbeatable combination. Work at this. Practice. Give yourself time, but make it your goal to become a mindful eater and to reap the enormous benefits it brings.

Day №4   Morning

Salut! Did you have a restful sleep? I hope so! I also hope you are now beginning to look forward to these morning rituals, that you are enjoying their many benefits, finding that they are helpful in bringing about the changes you seek. Here are this morning's activities:

1. Chi Belly Massage

2. Morning Breathing Practice

3. Chi Body Massage

4. Fresh Start Question 5

5. Mindful Breakfast Practice

6. Mindful Warrior Walk

Chi Belly Massage

As usual, let's start the morning with your Chi Belly Massage. (Remember, you should still be in bed!) This exercise is an amazing way to clear the agitations and negative energies that can accumulate during the night. As you do it, gently massage away any sore or tender spots you find as you circle your body in the band between your sternum and slightly below your navel. Be gentle and loving as you conduct your self-massage—this exercise should be, above all, a healing act of practical kindness.

Morning Breathing Practice

You learned this practice two mornings ago. Refer back to the instructions, if necessary, and remember that the trick lies in breathing "to" your head and "to" your toes to reintegrate mind and body.

Chi Body Massage

Okay, now move to the edge of the bed for your Chi Body Massage. In addition to its primary purpose of clearing stagnant chi, this practice also greatly improves circulation. In winter, especially, it is an effective way to improve blood flow within the body, the extremities in particular. If you suffer from morning stiffness of limbs and joints, you will find it a great comfort as well.

Fresh Start Question 5

Time again for some practical reflection. Take a pen and paper and write your answer to the following question:

> *What physical activities will I do to build on my vibrant new energy?*

Take some time to consider: Now that you are in the process of revitalizing your core physical self, what body-based activities will you engage in to help you cultivate your physical body in the physical world? Were you once a swimmer, a jogger, a dancer? Has it been years since you engaged in such an activity? Well, now is the time for your comeback! Make this your opportunity to build on the reconnection to the body you have initiated this week.

In addition to my wellness practice, I still teach yoga, water aerobics, dance, and weight training for the many benefits and joys they bring to my life. As a Pisces, I need to engage with water because it helps me release accumulated toxins and negative energy. But now the question is, what body-based activities are key to *your* physical health and wellbeing? Remember, balanced physical exercise is the key. Whatever activities you choose, make sure they benefit all three of the major fitness criteria: flexibility, strength, and endurance. Pick up that pen and start a list of the physical activities you know you need. Whatever is physical and enjoyable to you, get it down on the page: inventory the best ways for you to return to the physical, to renew your body and your self.

Mindful Breakfast Practice

As you eat your breakfast this morning, try to increase your eating awareness. Since awareness begins visually, take a good look at your food before eating it. What does it look like? If you are having cereal, for example, take a moment to notice its textures and colors before beginning to spoon it into your mouth.

When you actually eat, give yourself some time to experience the actual sensation of the food on your tongue, against the top and sides of your mouth. The aim is to fully engage your senses in the act of eating. How does your food smell? What do you hear when you chew it?

This morning, draw on all your mindful eating techniques to further cultivate your new orientation to food and eating. Stop after five bites to take three deep breaths. Eat some more, of course; you need this food to provide your body with the energy it needs for the coming day, but don't forget to answer your food awareness questions to bring about clarity and establish intention: What am I doing by eating? How do I want to feel? What do I actually need from this food?

As you eat, aim also to broaden the spectrum of your awareness. Feel, for example, the nutritious air as you breathe it, notice how it inflates your belly like a balloon—air is also sustenance, is it not? Who knows, the more you fill yourself with precious oxygen, the less food you might actually need!

Make each meal an opportunity to savor and meditate upon the gift of food in your life. Be thankful for whatever it is you are now eating, its sustaining gift to you this day. Move beyond taking its source and origin for granted. Recognize that what you are putting into your body likely (hopefully!) came from the earth, grew out of the richness of its soil. As such, your meal connects you and your life to the earth, to its winds, its waters, to the sun that makes all things possible.

Mindful Warrior Walk

Yesterday was your first experience of mindful walking. Today, on your walk to work, or on your lunch hour, or whenever you have the opportunity, add this new element to enhance your mindful walk.

After establishing your awareness of the simple and singular experience of placing one foot in front of the other—that absolutely commonplace act that goes entirely unnoticed—incorporate these affirmations:

- As you step forward to place your right foot down, as you "kiss the earth" with it, say *I can.*

- On your next step, as your left foot reaches forward and itself descends to kiss the earth, say *I do.*

- As your right foot comes forward to again kiss the earth, say *I will.*

- As your left foot again extends forward, as it has done thousands of times before and will willingly do for thousands more, exclaim *Yes!*

Let your *Yes* be primal! Let it affirm your life in this world, of the rightness of your existence. Let it affirm your commitment to your own well-being, and to the concrete actions that are bringing it about!

If you are so inspired, speed up your walk some and, while maintaining awareness, use *I can, I do, I will, Yes!* in an improvised chant or song. Draw upon the energy you feel in your limbs as you walk, chant, sing. Infuse your song with the same energy that powers your legs; feel their muscular strength. You are strong, are you not! This is your power: make it the foundation for your courage, use it to create the day you deserve and desire, use it to do what you need to do today, in the way you wish to do it. Perhaps you have never before thought of it, dear reader, but your body is a deep well, a fountain of nearly limitless energy. Draw upon these forces as you need them—they will make of you a warrior! Be thankful for these gifts; such thankfulness will feed and replenish them. Have an amazing day, my friend!

Remember, you possess enormous strength. If ever you begin to doubt it, stand up and walk—let your body remind you!

Tip of the Day
FOOD CRAVINGS

Today I would like you to pay particular attention to any and all food cravings you may have. If it is lunchtime and you are hungry, wonderful—enjoy. But there may be other points in the day when you begin to crave food, or a particular food: analyze the situation, establish the cause of your craving: what event, thought, or emotion triggered it? If you can begin to see causal links between your emotional life and your food or beverage cravings, you are well on your way to changing your eating habits—awareness precedes change! And don't forget that you now have the tools for dealing with these issues. Use those finger-grab and breathing exercises to dissolve any angers, frustrations, or disappointments that arise. The best of all possible days! Victory to you!

Day №4 Evening

How was your day today? Were you able to cultivate greater awareness of your body? Did you practice mindful eating? Mindful walking? I hope so, dear reader. Continuity of practice is the key to change!

Let's begin the evening's healthful rituals by using the arm swing to clear away any and all negative energies and agitations that may have arisen over the course of the day. Here are our activities:

1. Evening Cleansing Rituals: Arm Swing and Spinal Cord Breathing

2. Sound Therapy: Fourth Healing Sound

3. Finger Therapy: Ring Finger Grab

4. Starlit Sky Meditation

Evening Cleansing Rituals
ARM SWING AND SPINAL CORD BREATHING

As you do your arm swing exercise tonight, pay special attention to the sensations in your arms. Imagine them as heavy ropes hanging at your sides. When you sigh in relief at the top of every swing, make it loud and emphatic: although it may alarm the neighbors, this will greatly aid in releasing tensions. Aim to release all the emotions from the framework of the mind-body; aim to cleanse your body of negative energies and replace them with peace and calm.

After your ninth round, immediately move into your spinal cord breathing exercise, using the sharp HA sound for deep release. Generate it from Dan Tiem, your body's nexus of power at the belly's center.

Then take a little time to concentrate on the sensations in your body, feeling the rejuvenating power of fresh, vibrant chi coursing through your torso and limbs. If your body feels looser, as it should, celebrate its liberation from stress and anxiety.

Sound Therapy: Fourth Healing Sound

Tonight we move to the fourth healing sound, an extended HAAAA, which activates the heart and dissipates its associated energies of sadness, hurt, and grief: concentrate on replacing them with love, joy, and happiness!

Begin by sitting with your feet flat on the ground. Take a deep inbreath for four counts. As you exhale, make the HAAAA sound. Elongate the sound, ideally for eight counts. Repeat five times. Meditate on the emotions of love and joy, drawing on your memory if this helps you generate them. Finish by sending smiling, joyful energy down to your heart in loving appreciation for its precious life-giving function.

Finger Therapy: Ring Finger Grab

Choose now the ring finger of your left hand. Like the heart, it is intimately connected to the emotion of sadness. Gently wrap it with the fingers of your right hand, holding it until you feel a pulsing sensation. Imagine, then, all your sadnesses melting away, being absorbed by your ring finger. Smile in appreciation and gratitude.

Starlit Sky Meditation: An Introduction

Over time, losing sleep can significantly reduce one's quality of life and ability to perform effectively. And often we're not even aware we aren't getting enough rest. In one study, people who slept less than six hours a night for two weeks reported that they felt "only slightly sleepy," yet in performance diagnostics, they tested as poorly as those who had been sleep deprived for days. More ominously, perhaps, a 2003 study from Stanford University Medical College established causal links between disrupted sleep and cancer, suggesting that nocturnal hormone function, important in protecting against such cancers, was significantly impaired. For this and myriad other reasons, regular, restful sleep is basic to general health and well-being. This meditation will help you fall asleep more easily, turning off the chattering mind that is often still consumed by the stresses and distractions of the day. Shutting down the conscious mind not only helps you fall asleep more quickly, it also lets the subconscious mind begin its essential deep work of processing and resolving outstanding issues and emotions.

Starlit Sky "Sleepfulness" Meditation
FOR RESTORING RESTFUL SLEEP

Lie comfortably in any position you like. Begin your calming process by practicing the 3Cs.

You have, no doubt, been working hard. You may, in fact, still be feeling many of the day's pressures and concerns. Tell yourself that this is not the time to worry about them. This is evening, a time to let go. Pack all your troubles, duties, and responsibilities away in a box. Take as much time as necessary to do this. Now take the box and put it outside the door. Your mind is now free of such concerns.

You are now in a safe and quiet place. Let your breath dissolve into space and imagine floating in a starlit sky. Take your bed with you, if you want. As you float amidst the millions of stars that fill the sky, surrender to the benevolence of the night. Let darkness envelop and absorb all the events of day. Casting off your worries to the all-encompassing night, you feel weightless, relaxed, without the least concern. From this wonderful floating vantage point, look for shooting stars, watching as their bright trails streak by.

Begin now to seek deeper space. Let your mind penetrate the darkest reaches of the universe.

Don't worry about whether you are sleeping. Don't worry about the time. These things, all things, are unimportant. You are concerned only with surrendering your body to space. Here it is calm. Here it is still. Here there is no fear of wakefulness. Here there is no fear.

Think now to yourself:

I give myself permission to rest.
I trust tomorrow will be a good day.
I will wake up feeling refreshed, clear, focused.

My clients and friends have had wonderful success with this meditation. Use it anytime you have trouble falling asleep. The more you practice this meditation, the more powerful it will become. You can always return to the peace of the starlit sky!

Until tomorrow, my friend, sweet dreams—and *bonne nuit*!

Day №5   Morning

Good morning! I hope you slept soundly, dear reader. Did you use the Starlit Sky meditation last night? Even if you find it easy to fall asleep, to get the benefits of a truly restful sleep, give this amazing visualization a try this week. You are still in bed, I hope! Are you ready for your morning massage? Let's begin:

1. Chi Belly Massage

2. Morning Breathing Practice

3. Chi Body Massage

4. The 3Cs and Screening Room Practice

Chi Belly Massage

You are enjoying your morning routines by now, I hope. Soon you will find it nearly impossible to begin your day without them. I have been doing them many years now and I cannot imagine getting out of bed without first energizing myself from the comfort of my own bed. As is a Fresh Start morning tradition, complete your Chi Belly Massage—if you find any blockages (sore or tender spots), give them some extra loving attention.

Morning Breathing Practice

This morning I shall show you a new chi breathing technique, a highly effective means of activating and re-energizing your body. This morning you will initiate this practice lying down in your bed, but in the future you will do it outdoors where, with practice, you will learn to actively harness the energy of the sun by bringing its infinite restorative powers to the vessel of your own body.

1. Begin by holding both hands about five inches away from your belly.

2. Take in a great in-breath, drawing it into your belly so it expands outward.

3. Exhale.

4. Take in another great in-breath, this time imagining that within your belly you possess a small, radiant sun of your own.

5. Exhale fully, making sure your belly compresses, and visualize the radiant energy of your own internal sun turning into liquid gold, spreading its warmth out to meet your joined hands.

6. Take another great in-breath, and as you do so, pull the golden liquid of your radiant sun back from your hands to contain it entirely within your belly.

7. Complete nine cycles: inhale to pull radiant energy into the belly, exhale liquid energy to meet hands . . . do this nine times.

Such a visualization can take some practice. But once you get the knack of this exercise, you will go beyond imagining this radiant golden energy: you will be fully experiencing its power, the energy of the chi life force.

Chi Body Massage

Remember to sit up on the edge of your bed and to be vigorous in the workout you give your body. Get that blood flowing! Activate that chi so you will have a ready supply throughout your day!

The 3Cs Meditation and the Screening Room Practice

Let's cap off this morning's rituals with the 3Cs and the Screening Room. You should feel quite comfortable with both these essential Fresh Start exercises by now. Have the 3Cs become virtually automatic? Do you find yourself reflexively slipping into them at difficult moments during the day? Are your visualizations in the Screening Room becoming more concrete, more vivid? Remember, here you make your manifest your imagined and desired future, so make this all-important reconditioning activity your absolute highest priority.

. . . .

Finished? Wonderful! You have now re-energized the body and calmed and grounded the mind. What a superb way to begin your day. Enjoy it!

Day №5   Evening

Good evening! Tonight you're going to put all those individual exercises together to complete the whole chi puzzle—don't tell me you doubted they would ever fit together!

1. Evening Cleansing Rituals Combined: Wrist Shake, Arm Swing, and Spinal Cord Breathing

2. Sound Therapy: Fifth Healing Sound

3. Finger Therapy: Baby Finger Grab

4. Victory Count

Evening Cleansing Rituals Combined
WRIST SHAKE, ARM SWING, AND SPINAL CORD BREATHING

Here's how it goes: wrist shake (both directions), to arm swing (remember your sigh of relief), to spinal cord breathing (remember the HA sound), all repeated nine times If you're not sure you'll recall the details, take a moment now to review the instructions.

You're finished? Wonderful. Take this moment to stand perfectly still and enjoy the dance of the complementary yin and yang energies at the root of the chi life force. See if you can discern them: yin is the masculine energetic force radiating from the earth and flowing to you through the agency of your feet and legs; yang is the feminine energy of the sky flowing to you through the portal of the head. Feel these two forces within the mediating vessel of your own body. Regulating that equilibrium is the ultimate balancing act! Turn now to Dan Tiem (your energy nexus, located at the navel) and see if you can draw in and blend each of these two energies within its circumference. Keep working at it! You want to feel profoundly centered? This is how! Smile at this blissful experience. Congratulations, dear reader!

Sound Therapy: Fifth Healing Sound

Tonight we move to the fifth healing sound, RUUUU, which resonates with the spleen and helps dissipate the energy of depression and lethargy and replace them with excitement and enthusiasm. RUUUU is also an excellent aid to digestion, so don't be afraid to use it after lunch today (if you are in a fancy restaurant, expect a visit from the maitre d').

Begin by sitting with your feet flat on the floor. Take a deep in-breath for four counts. As you exhale, make the RUUUU sound. Elongate the sound, ideally for eight counts. Repeat five times. Meditate on the feeling of enthusiasm and excitement, drawing from your past if this is helpful. Finish by sending radiant, enthusiastic energy down to your spleen (upper left side of the abdomen, below the ribs) in appreciation for its cleansing function.

Finger Therapy: Baby Finger Grab

Choose now the baby finger of your left hand. In the Chinese system this finger is linked to exhaustion, distress, trying too hard. Gently wrap it with the fingers of your right hand, holding it until you feel a pulsing sensation. Imagine, then, all your distress and discouragement melting away to be absorbed by your baby finger. Smile at this experience in appreciation and gratitude.

Victory Count

CLAIMING VICTORY

Take some time now to sit with pen and paper. Write your successes down on the page so you can finally begin to recognize them and claim the victories that so often go uncelebrated. Remember, a success is something you have done well. Claiming success may take some effort, because we rarely think about what we do successfully; instead we focus on our mistakes, our errors, our inadequacies. If you are struggling to think of more than a few victories, try this: substitute yourself for George Bailey (the Jimmy Stewart character) in the movie *It's a Wonderful Life*.

What positive impacts have you had on the lives of those who love you? What would people who know you well say if they were celebrating you? There, you see, your victories could fill a book!

After you have written a fairly sizeable list, take a moment to bask in these accomplishments. You really are something after all, aren't you? Now do yourself a favor and carry this list with you for a few days (especially if you are likely to forget it by tomorrow morning). Make a habit of remembering both your past and your present successes. Stop taking yourself for granted, for heaven's sake! It's not a sin to celebrate yourself, you know!

Take those victories to bed with you tonight!

Day №6   Morning

Good morning! Still in bed, I hope! (When's the last time somebody said that to you?) Shall we begin?

1. Chi Belly Massage

2. Morning Breathing Practice

3. Fresh Start Question 6

4. The Lighthouse Meditation

Chi Belly Massage

As you do your Chi Belly Massage and morning breathing practice, consider that these activities have the same essential function as brushing your teeth and showering each morning. Just as you find it necessary to clean your "outsides," you'll find the same is true of your "insides." If you love the feeling of your fresh clean skin after a shower, for example, cultivate a similar appreciation of fresh clean organs! And believe me, my friend, the Chi Belly Massage is an organ cleanser *par excellence*! So cleaning your outer body is, yes, of course, wonderful! But cleaning your inner organs—even better! One last incentive, in case you need it: my Tao master told me that the heat created by the Chi Belly Massage helps melt away fatty tissues!

Morning Breathing Practice

You are probably pretty adept at breathing "to" your head and toes by now, so let's add another element to this visualization. As you breathe to the top of your head, imagine your breath as a sparkling golden light. Watch as it fills your entire head with radiant inner sunshine, pure energy. Imagine it awakening your mind to deeper clarities, insights, and wisdoms. As you do, meditate on the fact that the mind does not distinguish between what is actually experienced and what is imagined—think of the apparent reality of dreams, for example. Meditate also on the wisdom of the statement: *act as if you were and you will become.*

The mind is indeed a powerful thing, dear reader. In opposition, it limits possibilities; as a friend and an ally, it manifests them. Make of your mind an ally. Believe!

Fresh Start Question 6

Time now for some practical reflection. Take a pen and paper and write your answer to the following question:

How will my life be different with my vibrant new energy?

Take time to consider: Now that you are eating with greater awareness and intention, now that you are generating more positive chi (while ridding yourself of stagnant chi), now that you are using effective techniques to dissolve stress, now that you are doing all these new things, what do you intend to do with your newly energized and balanced self? Surely you are feeling more enthusiastic, more alive these days, so why not begin to imagine those things that were once unimaginable! How about ballet or jazz classes? Perhaps returning to school, or taking that test and trying for that promotion, perhaps taking that writing class, finally starting that book. Or how about that trip you've always wanted to take? Hey, even if you want to change nothing, even if you just want to more fully enjoy what you have: wonderful! Whatever it is, get it down on the page—this is the first step in making dreams real. Move them from your head onto the page, from the page into the world.

The Lighthouse Meditation
TO RESTORE HEALTH AND WELL-BEING

Calm yourself with the 3Cs. Sit comfortably. Breathe deeply.

Think about any places in your body that are burdensome, bothersome—anywhere at all. Perhaps a limb or muscle, perhaps an organ or an area of the chest or head.

Bring your awareness to this area now. Accept such discomfort, such pain, without accepting it as a judgment upon yourself. It is not you—it is simply a part of the body that has suffered some kind of trauma. Instead of worrying about its causes or its cure, just be *with* the discomfort right now, at this very moment. Become aware of the borders of the affected area, where it begins, where it ends. Examine the discomfort or pain itself: is it sharp or dull? Throbbing or piercing? Hot or cold? Study it without reacting to it.

Now move your awareness to your heart. Imagine at its center a luminous diamond. As you bring your full awareness to the diamond, it becomes larger, clearer, more sparkling. It radiates pure, almost blinding light.

Now, taking a minute to do so, focus the light into a beam. Step back in your mind's eye to see yourself now as a lighthouse, your heart sweeping a powerful beam of light through the darkness.

Now send this beam of light through your own body, illuminating the dark areas that afflict you, wherever there is discomfort, pain, disease. Imagine the beam dissolving those blockages. Imagine its benevolent light cleansing and revitalizing the surrounding tissues.

Now send your healing light beam throughout your body. Use it to scan all your tissues and sinews, bones and muscles, organs and extremities. Send the light everywhere, into every section and every corner of your body. You are the keeper of the lighthouse, keeping everything safe, illuminated, vibrant, and healthy. Watch as it sweeps away every obstacle and impediment to vibrant health, melting illness and dissolving pain.

Think to yourself:

My body was created by infinite intelligence.
My subconscious mind knows how to heal me.
It is now transforming every cell of my body, making me healthy
    and whole.

Your body's regenerative potential is infinite, dear reader. Help your body heal itself: focusing the beam on troublesome areas will serve to focus your body's restorative energies.

Day №6   Evening

I trust you had a good day! If it was not the day you had hoped for, all the more reason to engage in your Fresh Start cleansing rituals to find peace and calm once again. Tonight's activities:

1. Evening Cleansing Rituals Combined: Wrist Shake, Arm Swing, and Spinal Cord Breathing

2. Sound Therapy: Sixth Healing Sound

3. Finger Therapy: Combination

4. Emergency Release Therapy

Evening Cleansing Rituals Combined

WRIST SHAKE, ARM SWING, AND SPINAL CORD BREATHING

If you haven't done so already, try the whole sequence by heart, without glancing at the book. Once you get the combination down, you can do it in practically no time at all. Remember, nine repetitions for each set.

Sound Therapy: Sixth Healing Sound

Tonight we move to the sixth healing sound, EEEEE, which activates the triple warmer. (Remember that? It's the energy meridian associated with digestion and also with discernment and acceptance.) Begin by sitting with your feet flat on the floor. Take a deep in-breath for the count of four. As you exhale, make the EEEEE sound, elongated ideally for the count of eight. Repeat five times. Meditate on the emotion of acceptance, drawing on your past if that helps. Finish by sending accepting energy through your entire torso in loving appreciation of this healing moment. Smile at the experience of complete well being and yin–yang balance.

Finger Therapy Combination

Until tonight we've been practicing single finger therapy, but tonight and from now on, you will complete the combined set. Hold each finger for one minute, beginning with the thumb—and be sure to cultivate awareness of pulsation. Review the fingers and their associated energies:

- *left thumb:* reduces worry and helps combat smoking, nail biting, and cravings

- *left index finger:* combats fears and reduces back pain

- *left middle finger:* helps with anger and manifests patience and kindness

- *left ring finger:* dissipates sadness, also helps with asthma

- *left baby finger:* dissolves exhaustion and distress, also good for the heart

Emergency Release Therapy

When we have a sudden emotional crisis, the body's energy is trapped, blocked from circulating or dissipating. (Dr. Todd Sinett has analyzed the links between emotions and body ailments in his book *The Truth About Back Pain.*) At times like these, these energy traps need unblocking. A physical intervention is often required.

One of my clients had an ongoing problem at work: she was intimidated by the sound of her boss's voice. Upon hearing it, she lost her calm and her concentration, and it was affecting both her well-being and her work. She tried this emergency release therapy every morning and evening, and after just a week, she was able to completely neutralize her emotional responses to her employer. She finally began to enjoy her job and to do it effectively. If you suffer from similar responses in your work or your personal life, I urge you to keep this emergency release technique handy and give it a try!

1. Begin by rating your level of distress on a scale of one to ten (one = no distress, ten = extreme distress).

2. Using the index and middle fingers of your dominant hand, tap seven times each on these spaces:

   - between your eyebrows
   - cheekbone (to the side of your nose)
   - space between your nose and upper lip
   - center of your chin
   - under your collar bone
   - under your armpit (on the side of your choice)

3. Now, using the same two fingers, tap seven times on the side of each fingertip of the other hand (next to the nail). Skip the ring finger.

4. Now tap seven times on the underside of the same hand (the part you would use for a karate chop).

5. Now tap seven times in the space between the fourth and fifth knuckle (between ring finger and baby finger). As you do so, make a resonant humming sound for five to eight seconds (you may wish to hum "Happy Birthday").

6. Stop humming and count to five, then do another round of tapping and humming.

7. Visualize the face of a clock floating about two inches in front of your own face. Move your index finger clockwise around it. Keeping your head perfectly still, follow your finger's progress around the clock (twelve, one, two, and so on).

8. Repeat, moving counterclockwise this time.

9. Cover your eyes with cupped hands—bathe them in chi energy.

10. Rest your hands down on your lap.

11. Close your eyes. Take a moment to become aware of the peace-ful energy in your body. Take some gentle nurturing breaths.

12. Re-open your eyes and assess the situation from your new per-spective. Using the one-to-ten scale, rate your present distress level.

13. If your distress is still higher than you would like, or if it hasn't dropped at least three points, repeat the practice.

This is a most powerful technique, dear reader. If you suffer from frequent emotional crises, I urge you to use it to reap its benefits. As with all such techniques, the more you practice, the more powerful it becomes.

Day №7   Morning

Congratulations! You have made it to the final day of the second week of your Fresh Start. No small accomplishment, dear reader!

Let's wrap up the week by combining and reinforcing the many healthful body-based techniques you have practiced this week. Do all the following activities without referring to this book, trusting that they have been recorded by both mind and body. If you miss a section or a step, don't worry, move on to the next.

1. Morning Energizing Rituals Combined: Chi Belly Massage, Morning Breathing Practice, and Chi Body Massage

2. Mindful Eating Practice

3. Mindful Walking Practice

Morning Energizing Rituals Combined
CHI BELLY MASSAGE, MORNING BREATHING PRACTICE, AND CHI BODY MASSAGE

From today on, give yourself ten extra minutes for what we will call your Morning Energizing Rituals. Your body will love you for it: it will improve your digestion, concentration, attention, and physical energy.

First, energize your hands with the Chi Ball practice, if you wish. Then move right into the Chi Belly Massage, Morning Breathing Practice, and Chi Body Massage. With each exercise, your chi energy should become amplified. First generate it in your hands, then transfer its rejuvenating energy to your belly, head, toes, and torso.

Mindful Eating Practice

During breakfast this morning, once again train your awareness on your food *before* it is eaten! Take note of its shape, its texture, its colors. Stop after your fifth bite to re-establish clarity and intention. How hungry are you really? If you are rushing, slow down—eating should be a pleasure, remember, a chance to savor the gift of the food on your table. And remember, the goal of eating awareness is to install a new conditioning, a new orientation to food and diet. Change takes practice—meal time is practice time!

Mindful Walking Practice

On your way to work, once again establish a concentrated mindfulness of your body in motion. *Kiss the earth with your feet, touch the sky with your eyes.* Remember to use your verbalizations: *I can, I do, I will, Yes!* To these, you might today add: *I can, I create, I manifest!* Words with intention are words of power!

Day №7   Evening

I hope your day was filled with positive energy and awareness, dear reader. Tonight, we will review and reinforce your evening body-based rituals and practices.

1. Evening Cleansing Rituals Combined: Wrist Shake, Arm Swing, and Spinal Cord Breathing

2. Sound and Finger Therapy Combined

3. 3Cs and Screening Room Practice

4. Victory Count

Evening Cleansing Rituals Combined
WRIST SHAKE, ARM SWING, AND SPINAL CORD BREATHING

As you did this morning, move seamlessly from one activity to the next, focusing on maintaining awareness and continuity without worrying whether you are doing everything right or not. If you miss something, check back with the instructions only *after* you complete the entire set.

Sound and Finger Therapy Combined

You're right, there are six healing sounds, but tonight you will concentrate on the first five, to match the five fingers that are associated with the major organs (lungs, kidneys, liver, heart, and gallbladder). Begin by sitting with your feet flat on the floor. First take a deep in-breath for four counts. As you exhale, make the sound, ideally elongating it for eight counts. Repeat this pattern three times. Be sure to meditate on the positive emotions associated with each organ (see below), and to hold the corresponding finger at the same time.

1. **Lungs:** Make the SSSSS sound (like a serpent) while holding your left thumb. Imagine you are cleansing your mind of worries. Repeat the sound three times, then take three long, deep breaths, inhaling courage and peace of mind. Notice the pulse in the thumb before you move on to the next sound.

2. **Kidneys:** Make the sound of blowing out a candle while holding your left index finger. Imagine you are cleansing your mind of fears. Repeat the sound three times and then take three long, deep breaths, inhaling trust and faith. Notice the pulse in that finger before you move on to the next sound.

3. **Liver:** Make the SHHHH sound while holding your left ring finger. Imagine that you are cleansing your mind of anger and resentment. Repeat the sound three times, then take three long, deep in-breaths, inhaling patience and kindness. Notice the pulse in that finger before you move on to the next sound.

4. **Heart:** Make the HAAAA sound while holding your left ring finger. Imagine you are cleansing your mind of sadness and hurt. Repeat the sound three times, then take three long, deep breaths, inhaling love and joy. Notice the pulse in that finger before you move on to the next sound.

5. **Gallbladder:** Make the RUUUUU sound while holding your left baby finger. Imagine you are cleansing your mind of depression. Repeat the sound three times, then take three long, deep breaths, inhaling excitement and enthusiasm. Notice the pulse in that finger.

Practice this combination of sound and finger therapy together whenever you experience physical agitation and mental restlessness. You can even practice it on a noisy train or a bus. As you move forward on your path, keep in mind that such sounds are portable—you can take them and make them wherever you want. Next time you are walking down the street, for example, use this precious time to start making some healing noises. Be amused by any attention you receive. Channel the warmth and energy of this amusement throughout your body—as a friend of mine used to say, *never waste a positive emotion*!

The 3Cs Meditation and Screening Room

It's always great to conclude your Fresh Start rituals and exercise sessions with a combined session of the 3Cs and Screening Room. The clearance and cleansing achieved through your chi body-based rituals will give these two foundational activities even more power. Remember, you are engaging in the 3Cs and the Screening Room to create and reinforce the vision of change you identified in chapter 2. Trust in your vision. Trust that over time, it will become stronger and clearer. Trust in this process—*belief is the key to change!*

Victory Count

Tonight is the night for a small celebration—after all, you are fourteen days into your Fresh Start Promise—you are halfway through the program! You've absorbed a lot of new information and learned many new practices and techniques this week. Give yourself credit for your dedication, for your time and effort thus far. And credit yourself for keeping your mind open to philosophies and methods that may strike the Western mind as strange, esoteric, and even downright silly!

You are well on your way to lasting life change, dear reader. Be proud of yourself, will you! Now take some time to commit to paper these and the other victories of the last few days. Meditate on them as milestones on your path to transformation, sd as part of a greater trajectory of life change. Victory to you tonight! You've done some vitally important work this week. Tomorrow we enter our final circle of change, the world of the spirit. See you there!

Bonne nuit!

WEEK THREE
THE SPIRIT

I Will

I WILL

I Will

i will

I WILL

I Will

I WILL

Happiness is when what you
think, what you say and what
you do are in harmony.
MOHANDAS GANDHI

Who looks outside, dreams,
who looks inside, awakens.
CARL JUNG

Life in itself is an empty canvas, it
becomes whatsoever you paint on it.
You can paint misery, you can paint
bliss, this freedom is your glory.
OSHO

Believe those who are seeking the truth,
doubt those who find it.
ANDRÉ GIDE

Happiness is the meaning and purpose of life,
the whole aim and end of human existence.
ARISTOTLE

5

Awakening Your Spirit and Your *Joie de Vivre*

There once was a man desperate to know the meaning of life. He had taken and exhausted all the known paths. He had studied the original Judaic, Christian, and Islamic texts. He had filled his library with New Age titles, then filled his garage. He was so adept at yoga he could bend his body in twelve directions. He had traveled through the Kabalah, Zoroastrianism, Shinto, the Tao, and on through Buddhism.

Though all had unquestionable value, none had provided anything close to the clarity he desired. Surely, he thought, there must be someone who has the final piece of the puzzle. Somewhere, there is some wise and saintly soul who had discerned the answer he had somehow missed.

One day, taking the advice of one or two wise persons he had be-friended, the man decided to make one final pilgrimage to the land of the old masters, where the holiest of holies dwelled in mountain caves high in the world's most remote places. He traveled to that country, enlisted a guide, and began the arduous trek to a small monastery in the most obscure region of the Himalayas. On the last day he endured sub-zero temperatures, oxygen depletion, and a terrible blizzard. Un-daunted, he had suffered severely in his pursuit of the one great truth; surely he would now find his reward. Nearly frozen to death, unable to walk without the help of his Sherpa guide, he was led to the old master who sat serenely in the mouth of a mountain cave a mile beyond the monastery. With his grizzled, time-worn face, the monk looked an-cient, as if from another time.

After prostrating himself before the wisest of the wise, the man was instructed to sit. This he did, taking several minutes to summon the last of his strength and concentration before finally posing the ques-tion that had so consumed him. "Master," he said, "I am so happy to see you. I have searched for the meaning of existence for many years. I have traveled far and wide through many sacred texts, through many holy lands, until now, at last, I find myself in the presence of the one who must surely know." He paused. "Master," he began again, "please tell me, what is the meaning of this life?" The old master sighed, took a long breath, and smiled wisely. "Life is a fountain," he said.

Unable to believe his ears, the visitor was perplexed. Exhaustion, and then anger, crossed his face. He struggled to contain himself. "Please, master, I am in no condition for jokes. I beg of you, answer the ques-tion that has very nearly destroyed me." A puzzled look filled the mas-ter's face. His serenity drained away and his eyes filled with uncertainty. "So let me get this straight," he said. "Life isn't a fountain?"

· · · · · · · · · · · · · · · ·

Welcome to chapter 5 and the third week of your Fresh Start. This week we move to the spirit, the heart and soul of the human experience! If you are expecting some ultimate truth, I'm sorry, but I may disappoint you. The guiding truth here is that the search for ultimate answers is a solitary journey. (Were I to begin to provide them, you would be wise to put down this book immediately.) Big answers to even bigger questions? You won't find them here. That is your own work, and it will emerge from your own journey. Instead, I propose to give you something even more valuable: some questions, exercises, and meditations that have helped many of my clients reawaken, reconnect, and make their own way to the heart of the human spirit, to that wellspring of life's deeper joys.

Awhile back, I was on an early evening flight to New York. It had been a long day. I was tired and wanted only to return to the comfort and familiarity of home. After an exchange of pleasantries with the man seated next to me, I settled into my window seat, pulled out a magazine, and absent-mindedly flipped through the pages. A half hour into the flight, I glanced out the window. My eyes fell on the most stunning sunset I have ever been blessed to witness. From thirty thousand feet, the cloud layer was a gently tumbling sea, the crests of its waves feathered silver and gold, the evening sky above deepening into cobalt blue. To the west, the cloud-ocean glowed orange and red. Farther still, at the horizon's edge, was the most spectacular sight of all: though the sun itself was hidden, the clouds radiated crimson and violet. The vision was so surreal, so dazzling, so electric . . . it held me fast in its splendor. My body resonated to its fire; my mind resonated to this true benediction.

Such a blessing on such a difficult day! Moments before I had been a tired, distracted traveler thinking only of the comfort of bed. Now my spirit vibrated with the energy of one of nature's greatest gifts.

Now for the sad part of the story—at least for me. The man beside me had hooked himself up to some gadgets as soon as the seat belt sign had been turned off. With his iPod on, BlackBerry activated, he had been nimbly texting with impressive speed. Though he was completely immersed in his activities, the alertness of my gaze had caught his attention. Curious to see what so entranced his fellow passenger, he joined his gaze briefly to mine. "Astonishing, isn't it?" I suggested, venturing, in that basic human impulse, to share an intensely beautiful moment. By the time I turned to see his response, he had already returned to his work. Without glancing up again, he said, "Oh yeah, that's really something."

I was astonished, and I still am, that this sky of unique beauty could not hold the man's attention for even a moment. Such a gift, such a sunset, I may never see the likes of again. For him—postcard pretty perhaps, worthy of a quick glance, perhaps even less. Who knows. Whatever it was, it was certainly not the moment I experienced. Now I don't know the man, don't know the kind of day he had, the pressures of his life; for all I know he may have been color blind. But even so, all I could do was sadly wonder. Seated side by side, we were a million miles apart. I couldn't help but think that it was the allure of his devices that kept him from appreciating, to even a small degree, such a magnificent gift of the heavens.

In the days that followed, I began to more actively note people's engagement with their technologies. Again and again, I witnessed a commonplace sight: the individual in a public space, surrounded by humanity, yet alone with a device. Are we now at risk of enslavement to the distractions of the objects of our material world? What is the price of this fascination? I began to wonder. Have we become so eletronically preoccupied that the inner life, the life of the human spirit, now seems quaint, dull, perhaps even naïve?

In our practice of life change, a relevant question emerges: Can we dwell in a vacuum of the spirit and yet expect to be fully joyful, complete human beings? There are, unquestionably, hazards in the deeper pools of human experience: undertows and currents can pull us down to sadness as easily as they can carry us up to joy and light. Yet on balance, aren't the treasures of the soul too compelling to ignore? Still, in increasing numbers and to an ever-greater degree, we are ignoring them. Are we even aware of the splendid depths of the waters in which we swim?

What have we given up, I wonder now, with our ever-increasing fascination with the external, with the object? Are we even beginning to lose the greatest gift that consciousness gives—the engagement of the inner self with the outer world?

Surely it is in the deeper waters of human experience that we gain access to the spirit. Consider, if only for a moment, the degree to which your daily interactions are mediated through a material object. From the car to the computer to the cell phone, from the digital this to digital that . . . how long is the list of such things you have used, now use, or dream of using to enhance your daily life? It is substantial, is it not? Between our work and our workouts, our home and our home life, I wonder if our daily engagements with the material object far outnumber and outweigh our encounters with others, with ourselves, with our body, mind, spirit. Are such relationships negotiable purely through the material?

How many, I wonder, have accepted the idea that happiness lies in the *object*? How many are blind to this growing dependency on the material as the means to happiness? After all, the fires of our material attractions are fed by a billion-dollar advertising industry presenting to us in ever changing, ever so skillful ways, a vast, glittering array of *things* we can't possibly live without, sustained by a trillion-dollar manufacturing industry churning out more and more of such *things*, then updating them and improving them so that every six months or so, our *things* become obsolete.

Having the *thing* doesn't bring that much happiness, does it? The process begins in desire. Oh, I need that *thing*. Oh, I wish I could have that *thing*. Oh, I must have that *thing*. Purchase brings a brief moment of joy: oh, finally I've got that *thing*. This joy is usually short lived. The feeling of possession is never quite as good as we'd imagined, is it? Sometimes we are actually disappointed, depressed—angry, even, that our *things* didn't bring the happiness we thought they would. Within a year or so, there is always another *thing*, a better *thing*, one that frankly makes our old *thing* seem suddenly quite valueless. More unhappiness: Oh, you only have that old *thing*? You poor *thing*. And on it goes, and do we ever learn?

It's a straightforward question, but surely it still bears asking: are our material goods, our *things*, making us happy, or are they, in fact, making us miserable? We are certainly becoming great consumers, becoming great buyers and collectors of *things*, but are we becoming better human beings? Are we collecting great human experiences?

Please understand, there's nothing wrong with *things*. I myself love *things*. They can be fun, entrancing, distracting. Occasionally, they even make our lives better. Besides, consumerism keeps the economy going and the economy creates wealth and wealth is distributed—well, to some degree at least—so that more people can have, well, more *things*. That's the way the whole *thing* works, right? The problem lies not in *things*, but in our expectations. If I expect some kind of lasting satisfaction, some meaningful happiness or deep joy from a material object, I'm setting myself up for disappointment, am I not? He who seeks deeper meaning in a shallow pool scrapes his nose!

Surely life's more basic joys arise primarily through the agency of the spirit. But how many of us have forgotten our spirits or, if we still remember, know how to use them to create the profound human experiences we all need and want? We've been focused on surfaces for so long now, we've neglected our deeper selves to such a degree that the spirit has, for many of us, become wafer-thin, wasted, malnourished—perhaps we should add it to the list of endangered species!

THE SPIRIT: A USER'S GUIDE

Isn't it time we realized that our pursuit of the material at the expense of the spiritual is one of the greatest mistakes we could possibly make? Let us unclutter ourselves of the outer, of the purely physical, of the device. Let us rediscover what is innate, human, and real! The benefits of such a pursuit are limitless. By foregoing the purely physical, we encounter the spiritual and rediscover our self, mind, body, and spirit. The moment we tap into the internal, into the vast power of the mind-body-spirit continuum, our boundaries extend beyond all horizons imaginable.

Will you join me now in a rediscovery of the spirit? Though I would not presume to tell you the meaning of life, or how to find it, I will suggest that without a rekindled sense of joy, openness, and wonder, we stand little chance of connecting with our spirits. Can a life disconnected from the spirit be said to be a life at all?

The final weeks of Fresh Start provide us with a splendid opportunity to go forward to the garden of the human spirit. It's a slow process, requiring imagination and patience and vision and kindness, but it's an absolutely worthwhile journey, perhaps the only one worth making. We are, after all, amazing, magnificent beings, are we not? Let us work with our own natural faculties, intuition, imagination, our own innate sense of wonder. These are the channels that lead us to true wisdom, spiritual knowledge, and *joie de vivre*. Surely it is through our capacities for joy, kindness, curiosity, and thankfulness that we rediscover how truly wondrous human life can be. Shall we go forward, then, and engage the spirit in the process of change?

ON THE NECESSITY OF JOY

I was once stranded on a very nearly deserted Bahamian island at a particularly severe Yoga ashram. I was studying for an entire month at this secluded center, hoping to gain my certification as an instructor. The regimen was Spartan: in bed by 8:30, up before the sun at 5:00, the day filled with diligent study and arduous physical exertions. After a week, I was, quite frankly, a resentful young French woman. Gone were the make-up, the jewelry, the beautiful skirts and tops I had specially purchased for this beach paradise. At registration, we were asked to store our own clothes and handed a coarse saffron tunic, instructed to button it to the neck. It chafed. I chafed. The baggy white yoga pants were the plainest, most unadorned, most uninspired garment I have ever worn. I bore my growing resentment secretly. Though each morning I joined the others in Sanskrit chants and prayers, my youthful heart was unhappy, my serenity disturbed. The teacher was stern, Teutonic, unforgiving. I had given up my French identity, my *joie de vivre* for what? Military life? If this was the path, I had grave doubts about reaching the destination.

Sometime during the second week, unable to sleep, bored and nearly paralyzed by ennui, I heard what seemed like distant drumming. Hardly thinking about it, I was out of bed, putting on the skirt and chic top that had been lying idly in the bottom drawer. I opened and closed the door of my cell oh so quietly and carefully made my way down the narrow path from the residences to the compound gate. It was locked. I climbed it (that yogic strength and flexibility was good for something!). Outside, the beat was louder, more resonant, infectious, and irresistible. At the far, far end of the beach, perhaps a mile down, I could make out a dim halo of light. Surely this was the source of the sounds that so enticed. I took off my sandals and, striding purposefully across the ocean-dampened sand, began my second pilgrimage.

The moon was nearly full, and its light danced across the sea. The breeze off the water was still warm, almost hot. I enjoyed my walk, but I had my eyes set on some greater, as yet undiscovered prize. Sooner than I had imagined, I was within sight of the island's other compound. Now, along with the pulsing rhythm of the music, came other sounds, a cacophony of human voices. Spying a gate, I approached it. It was enormous, a double-layered wrought-iron affair with a man in uniform behind it, impassively watching me. I slowed down as I approached him, looking through the bars in search of the mysterious source of human voice and song. I stood silently, uncertainly, for what must have been a full minute. "Are you from the yoga place?" the man finally asked. "Yes," I nodded. The door swung open, and the man's face warmed into a welcoming grin. "Welcome to Club Med," he said.

I could have danced all night. Seriously. That night I very nearly did. After the austerity of the yoga boot camp, my discovery of the island's other sanctum, a discotheque, was truly heaven sent, a kind of shangri la for the spirit. I felt exuberant, I felt alive, I felt French again. Every day that week and the next, I awoke at five, diligently practiced my chants, my songs. I learned the most complex and demanding of yoga postures, I studied the ancient texts, I listened to the discourses. In all this, I excelled—at times my master almost seemed pleased. Every night I jumped the fence, walked that long stretch of beautiful beach, and every night I came back for more. I regained entry to the garden, put grooves in the dance floor, mixed modern dance with ancient yogic postures, fed my body and filled my soul with life's simplest joys and greatest treasures—movement and music.

Without judgment, everything is perfect. I put this forward to you now as perhaps one possible answer to an age-old question: asceticism, or hedonism? Nirvana, at least for me in that moment, could only be found in both.

JOY AND JOIE DE VIVRE

"When you kiss me, heaven sighs," Edith Piaf once famously sang. The song was "La Vie en Rose," perhaps the most gloriously sentimental love song ever composed—certainly the most French. Piaf's song is about the sweetness of life in a lover's arms, the singing of which elevates the singer, the lover, and the listener. This celebration of life's splendid colors is a French tradition, of course. Long ago the French came to the conclusion, somehow, that their permanent state of being had to be joy, not despair. Perhaps it was to distinguish themselves from their neighbors, perhaps they were inspired by their superb wine, the richness of their food, perhaps in the days before television and other gadgets, one simply had to find pleasures in ordinary things. Who knows, it was so long ago, no one remembers. It was, in any case, a splendid decision, don't you agree?

In English, *joie de vivre* is loosely translatable as *feeling carefree*, but this definition is sorely lacking, I think. Being free of cares strikes the ear as somewhat superficial, one quality of which the French cannot be accused. There is no easy, no *facile* way of explaining what is in fact the quintessentially French attitude. Like anything of deeper value, it takes some time to explain.

In America, we have moments of happiness that lighten an otherwise mostly serious state. In France, on the other hand, we have moments of unhappiness that punctuate an otherwise joyful state. An important, life-changing difference! What we focus on expands and becomes reality. French culture and language encourage a constant appreciation of joy. *Joie de vivre* is a way of seeing, a lens through which the French view life's events. Because this lens is acutely sensitive to life's joys, *la vie en rose,* such joys magnify and multiply. Perhaps you see the immense value of this perspective, this perception of life. Not too bad, *non?*

I've noticed the difference that these opposing life-views make. While my French friends focus on what gives them joy, my American friends and clients often focus what causes them distress. The result is dissatisfaction (remember, what we focus on *expands*). Such people respond to dissatisfaction by thinking they need more good events, more good *things* to make them feel better. Many spend a lifetime pursuing this idea. When something unwanted occurs, it reinforces their perception that *life is* a struggle. For the French, however, such unwanted events are a given, a part of life, certainly, but only a part. The French say "*c'est la vie*" ("such is life") and move on, *sans rancor.* If a culture's language reflects its thinking, the French language leads one away from obsessive dissatisfaction toward the expectation, the magnification of joy, continual joy.

Okay, you're laughing at me now! *C'est bon,* enjoy this moment, laughter is good! You think I'm trying to tell you that the French are, on the whole, in the midst of one long and perpetual giggle—that they are deliriously happy as they stroll down the boulevards of Paris. Of course not. Being human is hard, no matter what culture, what country you're from. But consider, when the French are sad, they're having a bad day, not a bad life. If you ask, "*comment ça va?*" (how are you doing?), the worst you are likely to get in response is "*comme si, comme ça*" (like this, like that—so-so). The French attitude toward life seems to accept both the positive and the negative, agreeing that both are to be expected from life, that one should, therefore, be surprised at neither. There is, of course, also the helpful assumption that joy will follow sadness, either the next day or the next, and that even that joy will be punctuated by sadness, and so on. *C'est la vie.*

If you're thinking that this sounds Buddhist in its assumption that all things, all joys, all sorrows must pass, I am with you. Maybe the Buddha had a stopover in Paris, *pourquoi pas?* Why not?

If you can see that *joie de vivre* assumes and celebrates both life's joys and life's struggles, you can also see, perhaps, that it tends naturally toward balance, since acceptance creates equilibrium. Such an attitude does not naively see life through rose-colored glasses, since it also understands the importance of embracing the whole of life.

Where then, can it be found? Only on television, in songs, in books, in the movies? Quite the contrary. Its essential quality is that it exists in the ordinary details of everyday life. If you cannot find it here, it is not *joie de vivre*. This contrast sharply with American culture, which celebrates heightened joys, higher positive states that arise mostly through the exceptional, the unusual, the rare. This exclusivity of joy, to the French way of thinking, is counterproductive because it imposes limits on the possibility of joy, on the number of things in which joy can be found. Joy must be frequent if one is to cultivate and, most importantly, sustain *joie de vivre*.

In French life, such joy *is* common. Precious moments can be found in eating—good food helps, as you can imagine! They can be found in conversation; they can be found in a warm summer evening, in a clear winter morning, in a small success of an ordinary day, in the feeling of the body embracing another, in the sound feet make on the pavement.

Perhaps the most important thing about *joie de vivre* is that it is self-perpetuating, since even the knowledge of one's capacity for it becomes a source of *joie de vivre* itself. This is its genius: it feeds itself, sustains itself, amplifies itself. *Formidable, non? Joie de vivre* is, in short, an all-encompassing philosophy of life's deeper happinesses, it is the experience of joy, the recognition of joy and celebration. The French have made an art of what is universal, and you can too!

La Nouvelle Joie de Vivre!

Do you see what I am up to now? Americans have enjoyed so many things from France, yet we have missed the most meaningful one of all. I should like to finally import that greatest of all French products and production. (Yes, we have in America the Statue of Liberty—a gift from the French, you remember—and we have *liberté, egalité, fraternité*. We have the many Americans who went to France and came back much improved: Thomas Paine, Thomas Jefferson, Benjamin Franklin, Henry

Miller. We have Champagne, cognac, and superb wines. We have food, of course, starting with *pomme frites*. (And now alphabetically: aubergine, baguette, béarnaise, bouillabaisse, crêpes, cassoulet, coquilles St. Jacques . . .) We have such glorious artists as Claude Monet, Henri Matisse, Claude Debussy, Piaf again . . . You are getting the picture, *non?*

But what we in America do not have, what we have never had, and what we need most of all, is that exquisite French quality of *joie de vivre*. We can make it our own: *joie de vivre à la americain!* Why it has never made it to these shores, I cannot say. Existentialism made it, for heaven's sake! Perhaps *joie de vivre* simply doesn't travel well. Like a soufflé, it is *très fragile,* and if it hits turbulence over the Atlantic it arrives a dismal flop. Perhaps it was turned back time after time at Ellis Island, then later at JFK. But I've got wonderful news! I've checked with Homeland Security, and it's not yet on that list of banned French products! I've brought back a case of it, and I offer it as the final course of your Fresh Start, or French Start, perhaps we should say! So are you ready for *la nouvelle joie de vivre!*

Joie de vivre: un recipe

What are *joie de vivre's* essential ingredients? Let's begin with humor.

On Cultivating Humor

The most wasted of all days is the one without laughter.

E.E. Cummings

Laugh at yourself first. before anyone else can.

Elsa Maxwell

Laughter is the closest distance between two people.

Victor Borge

God is a comedian playing to an audience too afraid to laugh!

Voltaire

When is the last time you laughed—I mean *really* laughed? Has it been ages? As you know from how you feel when you are in it, laughter is one of life's greatest hits. It floods the body with warmth, melts tensions, and diminishes sorrows. At the cellular level, laughter is medicine, *un elixir par excellence*! There is, of course, the story of Norman Cousins (of French ancestry, no doubt) who cured himself of cancer by locking himself and his wife (for after all, laughter, like Champagne, is best when it is shared) in a New York hotel room with an immense collection of the funniest movies available. Physician, heal thyself? Cousins did by laughing away his cancer!

The most healing laughter of all, paradoxically, is the laughter directed at the self. This self-humor is a little tricky at first, since it requires complete self-acceptance, knowledge of the self as an imperfect but still completely lovable being who stumbles and falls, who sometimes acts a complete buffoon in pursuit of goals that, when seen in the clear light of day, may be laughable in themselves. The man who can laugh at himself is indeed the happiest of men! What is life, after all, but a kind of slapstick comedy, in which people fall over themselves and others, getting up but to fall again. With the self as the star of life's divine comedy, one can never be bored!

What does this take, this capacity to simultaneously live one's life seriously and humorously? Well, it takes the self-assurance that one can suffer one's own laughter and still survive, for one. It takes self-love, ideally unconditional self-love. It takes humility, I suppose, the idea that one is both more and less than the sum of one's pretensions. Viewed in this way, humor *is* love, the loving capacity for laughter at all things, above all oneself, as one makes one's way rather clumsily through life, often clueless about its ultimate purpose.

In the practice chapter that follows, I will give you some practical exercises for cultivating such laughter, such self love, for laughter is an excellent way to reconnect to the spirit. For now, consider that more humor in your life could only be good. Maybe all it requires is that you loosen the necktie of your seriousness just a little—it really can get too tight, can it not? Let's pull that tie right off—later on I'll show you how to use it in a striptease!

On Honesty, Honestly!

No legacy is as rich as honesty.
  WILLIAM SHAKESPEARE

What comes from the heart, goes to the heart.
  SAMUEL TAYLOR COLERIDGE

When you learn to laugh at life, and at yourself, even if only a little, you have made an excellent start in your journey to the spirit. It prepares you for your next challenge: honesty, for *joie de vivre*, like humor, requires the intention of honesty, the capacity to cut through illusion and self-delusion to find and accept things as they really are. This means expressing how we truly feel, which itself requires the courage to hold nothing back, to look into another's eyes without fear, without turning away. We intend to cultivate joy, not bitterness, not to misuse honesty as an excuse for anger, jealousy, envy, or malice, of course. Never, *mon dieu! Absolute* honesty is a liberation for both the sender and the receiver. If you want something from somebody, tell them directly. They will appreciate it, I can tell you. If you play games, deceive, strategize, manipulate, or wheedle, this irritates, or worse. We know this but we withhold and mask our aims and intentions anyway. Why? We are afraid we won't get it. Well, so what? If you don't get it, you don't get it! Is this the end of the world? I don't think so! As a friend of mine says: if you don't ask, the answer is always no. But begin with the self, for there is no greater liar than the one we see in the mirror. What are your real motives? You want to think you are right, you want to be *righteous*, think the other wrong. Nonsense. We all have motives, wants, and needs. We are all ego-driven. Admit it, it's okay, you know! So you want something, it's not a sin. You want it because it is going to give you pleasure. Wonderful! Nothing could be more natural. But be sure not to take what is not given, not to increase your pleasure at the expense of another's pain. Becoming more honest is another essential route to the garden of the spirit—in the next chapter I will provide you with some concrete exercises for making the journey.

On Curiosity, Wonder, and Openness

Curiosity has its own reason for existing. One cannot help but be in awe of the mysteries of eternity, of life, of the marvelous structure of reality. It is enough if one tries merely to comprehend a little of this mystery every day. Never lose a holy curiosity.

Albert Einstein

I can believe anything, provided it is quite incredible.

Oscar Wilde

If what Thoreau said is true, that many of us live *lives of quiet desperation,* I suspect it's because we have stopped wondering; we have become closed to the splendors of everyday life. The "ordinary world," as Monsieur Henry Miller reminded us, is far from ordinary. "Develop an interest in life as you see it," Miller wisely counseled, "in people, things, literature, music—the world is so rich, simply throbbing with rich treasures, beautiful souls, and interesting people. Forget yourself."

Wake up tomorrow and do something differently from the way you do it every day: that is my recipe for developing wonder. It's the perfect beginning toward openness, curiosity, and the deeper pools of the human spirit. The chief obstacle to seeing the extraordinary in the ordinary is repetition, *the same old, same old*. But it's not the things you see every day that are old, dull, boring. It's you, my friend, you who have made them so! Take a moment to see them again—take another, a closer look. Give the ordinary world another chance and you'll be glad you did. In the faces you see every day, there is a gallery of human beauty and wisdom and experience. Study them! Celebrate them. Learn from them. What about the natural light around us? Is it ever the same? Never! As artists have shown for centuries, the quality of light and, therefore, the world it illuminates, is never exactly the same. Spring, summer, fall, winter, August, April, January: never, ever the same. The approach of spring, the tiny buds emerging from branches, the progress of nature in rich soil of the earth—in spring the world is never still, not even for a moment. A daily walk in observation of the world will very quickly cure you of the notion that things remain the same. Cultivate your awareness of this and a reconnection to the world and the spirit will quickly follow.

Curiosity leads to curiosity, wonder to wonder. Open yourself as the flower opens each day to the sun. Have you ever wondered exactly what artists are up to? Here is a suggestion: read them, see them, study them, pay attention to them! The gift of the artist to the world is to help us *see again*, to defamiliarize what repetition and closed minds and hearts have made so familiar that we have become blind and numb to its beauty. France has a long tradition of supporting and nurturing the world's artists. In return, such artists have assisted the French in their mission to cultivate and sustain their *joie de vivre*, to see again and again, but always anew.

To get you started, I suggest you read "anyone lived in a pretty how town," a remarkable poem by that most remarkable of American poets, e.e. cummings, another who blossomed on French soil. It should be easy to find, and it's short. Its language is simple but surprising. If you don't want to struggle to find its meaning, don't! Forget meaning! Enjoy it for its sounds and its singularity, the play of its simple, child-like language. Be entranced!

When Cummings says ". . . and more and more they dream their sleep," could he be talking about us? Are we asleep? Will we miss his warning? Only if we continue to live as if every day were the same. Stop it, I tell you! Wake up! It's such a waste, is it not? Remember that the world's "up so floating, many bells down."

In the following chapter you will engage in practical exercises for cultivating your sense of openness and wonder. For now, please simply be open to the possibility that these lead you back to the spirit!

On Compassion

> I would rather feel compassion than know the meaning of it.
>
> **Thomas Aquinas**

> If you want others to be happy, practice compassion. If you want to be happy, practice compassion.
>
> **Dalai Lama**

Okay, so now I'm really pushing it, aren't I! Yes, I want you to be nice to others, to help them across the street. Come on, I know you can do it! Compassion stirs the spirit! Start with this, start by looking inside you, at yourself and your own struggle. Life is difficult, is it not? We are born and by age twenty or so, we're already beginning to die. It's really quite terrible, isn't it? We want love and can't find it, or if we do, it's not the love we thought we wanted. We don't become as famous or as rich as we'd like; our *things* aren't that pleasing. We watch our parents grow old and die, we follow so quickly behind. Misery? Nonsense—utter nonsense. That's simply the way it is: don't kid yourself. Acknowledge the fact that you're getting older, rounder, and probably none the wiser! Now, see the other as yourself. You think there are that many differences between you? If so, you are still suffering from illusions. Keep trying, you'll get it! If you can recognize that others struggle as you do, that others are, on balance, very much like you, that what separates you is largely the product of the ego's fantasies—then you are well on your way to compassion. You can see that the road is slippery, traffic is heavy, the lights don't always work, and the guy who just cut you off must be having a terrible day. The one who is angry suffers his anger far more than you do. (Remember the song "He Ain't Heavy, He's My Brother"? . . . You've got it, my friend!)

Compassion, once cultivated, is a very nearly divine state of being. Compassion, once you've got a good crop of it growing, nurtures the seeds of future compassion. Real, pure compassion, loving kindness to others, connects one to the spirit and instills an exquisite, peaceful feeling. No, not because you feel like a good person, a righteous person. If you're there, you're not there: keep trying! True compassion, once cultivated, liberates you from anger with others, from disappointment and frustration and irritation with others. Compassion transforms anger into love. So transformed, you free yourself, are free to love yourself more, have greater compassion for yourself. It's a win-win, you know. Drop this idea of selflessness, for heaven's sake! There is no greater depressive than the selfless, the one who sacrifices self-interest to help others (and no one more boring). This is a terrible mistake, I tell you. To love others you must first love yourself, to love yourself you must be happy. Begin to make yourself happy by having compassion for your self first. Suffering, you only spread suffering. (Horrible!) Have compassion not because your Savior said it would be a good idea and you would like to go to heaven. Have compassion because with it you can begin to save yourself, and saving yourself, you may be able to help others! Stay tuned for some practical, concrete ways of developing compassion and finding yet another path to the waterfall of the human spirit!

ON GRATITUDE AND APPRECIATION

Appreciation is a wonderful thing: It makes what is excellent in others belong to us as well.

VOLTAIRE

Let us be grateful to people who make us happy. They are the charming gardeners who make our souls blossom.

MARCEL PROUST

Okay, you're beginning to get it! Once you've cultivated the beginnings of humor, honesty, curiosity, openness, wonder, and compassion—don't worry, you'll find instructions for this *joie de vivre* recipe in the next chapter—then you'll surely be ready for the next stage, ready to give thanks, to cultivate appreciation. Things are far from perfect, I am the first to admit it. We weren't born with the bodies we would have chosen ourselves, or perhaps the parents, the children, the spouse—well, we did, after all, choose our spouse. But you see what I mean. Life is hard, but as the mother of a friend said, "It's a wonderful privilege to be born." This of it! This was not a given, friend. And even if it was, you might have been born as a cow, endlessly milked, a gazelle to be forever worried about the lion, a roach to be despised and poisoned, pond scum to be inert and bored. Things could be worse, remember that. Things could always be worse! And while this is a rather awkward route to thankfulness, consider that for things to get better, you may first have to recognize they could be worse!

Cultivate gratitude. Take inventory. What do you have? Your life, I think we've established! Your capacity for love, joy, and fulfillment is another. Human life is, above all, a magnificent potentiality. You have your health, I trust. (If not, I'm sorry, but perhaps you once had it; be thankful for that at least.) Begin by having a good look around you, look at the unbelievable suffering of others (have compassion as you do so, please). The man who thinks he is unluckiest of all is the biggest fool of all. You are reading this book? So, my friend, you can read! How wonderful for you. You have access to the greatest minds and imaginations in human history. You want to take this for granted? Ungrateful, aren't you! Do you know how many people can't read? You bought this book, did you not? You can afford to spend money on such idle pursuits as trying to make your life better? Millions can't. Millions must spend such money (if they've got it) on food, shelter, medicine (if they can get it). You are reading this by the light of an electric lamp? Another blessing, electricity! You think I'm kidding? Thousands of human souls can't simply flick a switch. You're getting the idea, right? It is a kind of blindness, a kind of absolute memory loss to be unable to find hundreds of things to be thankful for daily. We are such amnesiacs, don't you agree?

In this week's practice chapter I give you practical instructions for cultivating thankfulness as yet another route to the spirit. For now, accept that being grateful is simply a good idea, that it can improve your life. Start by getting down on your knees. Yes, an excellent position. Being prostrate is the appropriate physical posture for cultivating thankfulness, for it demands that most difficult of things, in particular for the French: humility. Only by cultivating humility can you become truly grateful, truly connected to the spirit. Look, I'll get you going. The fact of the matter is that while you are good, my friend, you aren't that great!

On Connecting to Yourself

Life is not about finding yourself. Life is about creating yourself.

GEORGE BERNARD SHAW

You didn't come into this world. You came out of it like a wave from the ocean. You are not a stranger here.

ALAN WATTS

As I have seen many times in my clients, connecting to the spirit creates a profound shift in mind-body alignment. It results in what I call full integration. Such a shift, when it occurs, feels for many like suddenly having more oxygen, as if they were finally breathing to the fullest, which they are. Life without spirit is, on the other hand, like breathing with only one lung. It is taking in and absorbing only a small portion of life's joy, pleasure, and experience. This metaphor of breath is appropriate, in fact, for though we lose it in English, the word spirit means breath—from the Old French *esprit* (naturally!)—which is in turn from the Latin *spiritus*, or *spirare*, "to breathe." Seen this way, spirit is what separates the living from the dead: no breath, no life. Full, deep life breaths (life experiences) center the self: such breathing replaces anxiety and worry with deeper, more positive energy and with a tangible link to all things, your self especially. Let's use one of those "perfect" days in life as an example. Imagine this day now—perhaps it was spring, the day warm, a palpable sense of the new filling the air. Everywhere you looked was beauty, flowers and trees in bloom. At this moment you probably felt that everything was perfect, everything was *just as it should be.* When you looked at this scene and at all its discrete elements, surely you experienced a charge, a "hit," as if you were wired to the world around you, as if the beauty of the environment were an electrical charge firing within your mind and body. All worries, all cares surely fell away on that particular day. At that moment there was no right, no wrong—all concerns, all arguments dissolved, unimportant, absurd even. You felt the pure energy of being, multiple bursts of joy in the heart, a child's innocence perhaps; maybe you even laughed out loud. How silly, how demeaning seemed the day's ordinary stresses and concerns. The *things* you thought you needed must have seemed paltry at that moment: you needed nothing, you were a fully integrated being. Your thoughts themselves were, perhaps, a kind of ongoing prayer in praise of being, in praise of the beautiful world and your life in it. You did nothing. You said nothing. You opened yourself as a flower to the sun, absorbing the day's radiant perfection. The path was clear—suddenly there was purpose and clarity and order to what may have previously been chaotic and meaningless. Such a day was a time of absolute connection to the spirit, a moment of pure inspiration—full integration with the spirit—a moment of complete enthusiasm (a word rooted in the ancient Greek *entheos:* "being with and inspired by God").

You've had those kinds of days, haven't you! Aren't they what life is all about? Now begin to imagine every day as such a day. It is possible, you know. Do you dare to believe it? Developing your deeper faculties, cultivating your inner receptivity to nature (your own and the world's), will help you have many more such days. It all begins with your willingness to have them.

My own first full experience of the spirit's bliss occurred when I was fifteen. It grew out of a spiritual crisis, in fact. I was living in Cannes with my grandmother, you remember her? That morning I awoke with the resolution that I would stop attending church. Since I was nine, my grandmother had been taking me to mass and confession. Reluctantly, I had been made to whisper my life's many crimes in a darkened chamber to a man I hardly knew. My problem was that I didn't feel particularly guilty of anything. Despite a devoutly Catholic upbringing, I remained unconvinced that I was a fallen creature, doubtful that I could be a sinner at all.

Sin made no sense to me. It was in absolute opposition to my nature, which, when unbothered by others, was absolutely free, almost entirely innocent. What was I to tell this priest on a weekly basis—that I ate too much chocolate, that I giggled and gossiped with my friends about the celebrities on television, that I often wished my parents would arrive and save me from my mean grandmother? If these were my sins, I was an unrepentant sinner.

Every week, I made things up, created lies for my ghastly little session, said the prayers I was given as an act of contrition, walked out of the church resentful, shamed, and angry. Bad behavior? Who was to tell me that my thoughts and wishes and desires were wrong? By the age of fifteen, I'd had my fill. That morning I sat down at the breakfast table and announced my intention to leave the church. Grandmother was appalled—she practically fell off her chair. Who was this girl to think she could simply walk out of an institution that had been the backbone of French life since time immemorial?

Grandmother scolded me severely. She said my nature was too free and my unrestrained *joie de vivre* would surely lead me down the devil's path. *Joie de vivre* existed for Grandmother, I suppose, but only as a heavenly reward for a pious life.

All day at school I was deeply disturbed. I was hurt by the bitterness of my grandmother's response, upset that I had, against my will, caused her pain, confused by the contradictions between what I felt to be true and what I was told was true. By the time the school day ended, I was entirely despondent. I was crying, inconsolable, a wreck. I had begun to think that Grandmother was right, that there was actually something wrong with my very nature. It seemed to me then that I would never be happy in this world and that my unhappiness would, in turn, cause me to do things that would lead to my damnation.

I was so upset. I knew I couldn't go home just then. Without thinking much about it, I turned and took a detour that probably saved my life—I made my way down to the water. The evening was probably not so different from any other in the early spring in the south of France— and yet it was. That May evening, a young girl went to the water's edge and was given the answer she so desperately needed.

Walking along the beach, I reviewed the questions that plagued me. Were Grandmother and the priest right? Was I by my very nature a sinner? Must I, then, rein myself in, suppress my desire to live life fully, subdue my true self? Was this God's plan? Did God want, above all, perfect behavior? And how could my grandmother and the priest know this?

I was now very nearly at the end of the beach, more thoroughly depressed than ever. By this time I had convinced myself that I was nothing more than a foolish, headstrong girl. What did I know about the world? Surely Grandmother and the priest and God had knowledge of many things that I did not. Dejected, forlorn, I resolved to change my ways and my thinking. Look at the pain I was causing my grandmother. I was a source of great unhappiness to a woman who had made so many sacrifices for me. Yes, clearly I was wrong, once again, dead wrong.

I turned and began to make my way back. I was very sad, of course. But life was sad, everyone said so. I made my grim way forward, resolved to respect and abide by the path set out for me. At this moment, everything changed. How and why, to this day I cannot be certain.

In the suspension of thought that followed my decision to change my ways, the true nature of the world raised itself up to persuade me otherwise, to convince me that I was wrong in my decision to change myself for the sake of Grandmother and Church and God. What can I tell you; how can I explain? As I walked I looked to the sky; it had started to deepen into night. To the west, it was turning pink and orange as it did nearly every evening at this time of year. Yet today was not typical. Today it seemed a very celebration of color (you see, now, how important sunsets have been for me). Here, where the blue waves of the Mediterranean met the white shores of Europe, I was filled with a reverence I had never felt before. Here was God's beauty, I knew then. This was God's church, perfect in itself. In the clarity of that insight, I knew that I was right, that my nature was right—knew that my ability to experience the splendor of God and nature was grace and holiness itself. For the first time, I became myself.

Perhaps the narrow path was right for some, for my grandmother and the priest, certainly. I was not to judge them—yet for me, the path was different. I resolved to love my grandmother twice as much as before, to accept her completely, yet not sacrifice myself in the process. This was God's will for me—this was my way. No matter how my life would unfold, I would be—and have been—faithful to that day's vision. I was right after all! *Joie de vivre* was right. God was right. We were *all* right!

· · · · · · · · · · · · · · · ·

When we do the spirit work we need to do, all defense mechanisms fall away. We become clear. We immerse ourselves in life, we lose ourselves to the moment, and so we return to the garden once more. Once inside, we become "*inter-esse*," meaning to be *among*, to be *concerned*, to *share* in the world, to sympathize, to be curious, to be *enthusiastic*.

This journey to the spirit is predominantly guided by the invisible. Spiritual beings trust and feel the gentle hand and voice of intuition; they are enthusiastic about life. They believe every day is filled with infinite possibility. They focus not on what the ego wants, but on what is for their highest good. They are filled and fulfilled by a life purpose, a mission; they are highly creative and imaginative; they have the courage to look at themselves and the willingness to transform their beliefs and attitudes. They love adventure and new people. Their connection to others is generous, is negotiated through kindness and joy. They show empathy and choose to uplift all those they encounter.

With such a profound shift, we become more accepting and less controlling, more flexible and less grasping, more peaceful and less troubled. We gain the freedom to flow with our emotions, to respond openly to situations, to communicate ourselves to the world. In other words, we become ready to engage and connect with others.

On Connecting to Others

Treat people the way that you would like them to be and they will become.
Friedrich Nietzsche

We are here to awaken from the illusion of our separateness.
Thich Nhat Hanh

You will soon discover that when you begin to make positive changes in your life, your relationships change, too. You will suddenly have compassion for difficult people, will find them *different*, but no longer *difficult*. Others are, after all, our greatest teachers—even when they don't know it themselves! Others teach patience, others teach understanding. With a strong connection to the spirit, all things change.

The really wonderful thing is that with your new connection to the spirit, you will begin to attract new and different people, others who are also invested in love, honesty, and integrity. Don't ask me how this happens—I really couldn't tell you. But it does, it simply does. You'll notice fewer pretensions and deceptions in your relations with people. Your new relationships will be more authentic, trusting, nurturing. Your *joie de vivre* will give you the energy surplus to negotiate all your important interactions with others. With it you will stop taking things so seriously, you will suffer less from the stings that do sometimes occur in human interaction. You will begin to see that others are imperfect, yes, but lovable nonetheless. You will see that their mistakes are the result of the conditions that shaped them, their childhoods, their natures, their own particular limitations.

Suspending judgment is the key to successful human relations. When you are "made to feel" badly around others, see that this is an ego-created illusion. People rarely mean to make you feel a particular way in their company; in fact, people can't actually make you feel anything. Don't give them this power; don't give them this responsibility. Only you can make yourself feel something. Your reactions to others make you feel the way you do, don't you know! Your reactions are yours—rooted in your own frailties, insecurities, limitations. Recognize this simple fact and you will have the key to a happy life! Stop blaming others and you will learn to love them.

This is vital: good nature and goodwill have tremendous power in human relationships and in the lives of others. People begin to glow when they are in the presence of another who genuinely wishes them well. Your positive attitude, your "happy" energy allows them to finally let down their guard. People blossom in nonthreatening environments. This blooming, when it occurs, is magical. People become glad of your presence, happier with themselves and how they feel in your company. This is magic, dear friend, absolute magic. Now glowing and blossoming, others will return the favor you have bestowed upon them, probably without even knowing they are doing so. They will return the love. At that moment you will find yourself on the receiving end of the sweetness of human kindness, fraternity, and warmth—and it is wonderful, simply wonderful.

· · · · · · · · · · · · · · · ·

So how can we sum up the importance of the spirit in the pursuit of life change? A deeper connection to the spirit helps us become the people we want to be: better, more open, more loving, more curious, more thankful, more honest, connected to the self, connecting to others. If you have found some wisdoms and small truths in this chapter, I am grateful, but

I am, of course, only a "hunter-gatherer" here. My debt, all our debts, in fact, are to those who came before us, who considered the same human circumstances we face today, and who put down the insights and knowledge they gained so that others might also learn and not only ease their misery but greatly enrich their lives. Please consider these wisdoms carefully, dear reader, for they can change your world completely. And remember, if we are to benefit from such wisdoms, we must begin to practice them.

Join me now to engage in a week of concrete, practical exercises and meditations to create joy and *joie de vivre* in your life. Forward in the spirit of *la nouvelle joie de vivre*, shall we?

My wonderful French artist friend Marie-Therese Ancellin wrote this for me . . . and for you. Let it be our own rousing anthem. Forward!

Joie de Vivre
Vivre la joie (Live the joy)
La joie de vivre (The joy of life)
Ivre de joie (Drunk from joy)
Ivre de vie (Drunk from life)
Joyeux de vivre de joie (How joyful to live with joy)
Vive la vie (Long life to life)

The Practice of Awakening Your Spirit

Did chapter 5 begin to awaken you to the many benefits of a stronger, clearer connection to the spirit? Did you find some appeal in the idea of a life filled with *joie de vivre?* I certainly hope so! You don't have to be French; it makes no difference if you've never even visited France. The only requirement is that you possess the desire to get more out of life, to enjoy the many small pleasures of everyday laughter, hope, love, and joy that make life truly worth living. And as for deepening your connection to the spirit, this too is straightforward: no metaphysics, no esoteric philosophies are needed. This too requires only an openness and desire for joy—and I have yet to meet someone who doesn't fit this bill! Life can be a celebration, if only we learn to sing a little. So shall we try a few notes now as we go forward to incorporate the spirit into our practice of change? Don't worry if your first few notes are off-key: the important thing is only that you raise your voice in song!

Like the other practice chapters of *The Fresh Start Promise*, chapter 6 will take you step by step and day by day through the new week of your life change program. Throughout these seven days you will continue to practice the techniques you began in Week Two and the foundational work you learned in Week One. To all these practices we will add a variety of exercises and activities to reawaken the slumbering spirit. Please note that you will do many of Week Three's activities not in your living room, not in your bedroom, but out in the world—for that is, after all, where we live and, therefore, where we must find our joy. The one thing I can assure you this week is that you will have loads of fun engaging in these new practices with your friends, family, and co-workers. Week Three is about awakening your curiosity and deepening your connection to yourself and others. It is about finding and then showing gratitude toward yourself and your life; it is about awakening your intuition, that profoundly human but often underused faculty; finally, it is about identifying the ever-present synchronicities in human thought, intuition, encounters, and events—the deeper fabric of reality that many of us suspect is there, but few of us firmly believe in.

Above all things, Week Three will be great fun, for after all, you are giving birth to the life-affirming spirit of *joie de vivre*. If you like, you may cultivate a French accent, pretend to be Maurice Chevalier or Edith Piaf. And look, if you can't quite believe that you are capable of such a fundamental shift in outlook, try it anyway and have fun in the trying. The willingness to attempt something new, something different, however silly, is in itself a form of openness and *joie de vivre*! By week's end, I promise you, you will be a believer!

The Fresh Start Promise
WEEK THREE DAILY SCHEDULE

DAY 1

Morning

Chi Belly Massage
Morning Breathing Practice
Chi Body Massage
Fresh Start Question 7
Four Ways to Awaken Dormant
   Curiosity

Evening

Wrist Shake, Arm Swing, Spinal Cord
   Breathing
3Cs Meditation Practice
Reflection: The Experience of the
   Day
The Screening Room Practice

DAY 2

Morning

Chi Belly Massage
Morning Breathing Practice
Chi Body Massage
Meditation: Diamond of the Heart
Three Ways to Connect to Yourself
Three Ways to Connect to Others

Evening

Wrist Shake, Arm Swing, Spinal Cord
   Breathing
Meditation: The Garden of the Heart
Victory Count

DAY 3

Morning

Chi Belly Massage
Morning Breathing Practice
Chi Body Massage
Fresh Start Question 8
A Few Ways to Laugh
Joke of the Day

Evening

Wrist Shake, Arm Swing, Spinal Cord
   Breathing
3Cs Meditation Practice
Golden Chalice Meditation
Garden of the Heart Meditation with
   Anchoring Hand

DAY 4

Morning

Chi Belly Massage
Morning Breathing Practice
Chi Body Massage
Three Ways to Show Compassion
   and Kindness
Mindful Warrior Walk

Evening

Wrist Shake, Arm Swing, Spinal Cord
   Breathing
3Cs Meditation Practice
Satellite Meditation
Reflection: Applying the Satellite in
   Your Life

DAY 5

Morning
Chi Belly Massage
Morning Breathing Practice
Chi Body Massage
Fresh Start Question 9
Three Ways to Show Gratitude and
  Appreciation

Evening
Wrist Shake, Arm Swing, Spinal Cord
  Breathing
Sound Therapy: The Six Healing
  Sounds
Mindful Eating Practice with
  Appreciation
Victory Count

DAY 6

Morning
Chi Belly Massage
Morning Breathing Practice
Chi Body Massage
Three Ways to Develop Your
  Intuition
Mindful Warrior Walk

Evening
Wrist Shake, Arm Swing, Spinal Cord
  Breathing
3Cs Meditation Practice
Night Walk Meditation

DAY 7

Morning
Chi Belly Massage
Morning Breathing Practice
Chi Body Massage
Three Ways to Experience Joie de
  Vivre

Evening
Wrist Shake, Arm Swing, Spinal Cord
  Breathing
3Cs Meditation Practice and
  Screening Room
Victory Count

Day №1 Morning

Bonjour! How did you sleep? Soundly, I hope! Congratulations on beginning the third week of your Fresh Start! You are something of a veteran now, but it is important that you continue both the core practices of Week One and the body-based practices of Week Two. These, together with this week's spirit-based practices, make up the essential Fresh Start program. Working together, the rituals and exercises of your mind, body, and spirit work will move you inevitably forward. As we know by now, it is continuity of practice that makes your new conditioning permanent: this principle lies at the heart of your Fresh Start. Here are this morning's activities:

1. Morning Energizing Rituals: Chi Belly Massage, Morning Breathing Practice, Chi Body Massage

2. Fresh Start Question 7

3. Four Ways to Awaken Dormant Curiosity

Morning Energizing Rituals

CHI BELLY MASSAGE, MORNING BREATHING PRACTICE, CHI BODY MASSAGE

So this week, and on into the future, start your day with these three, which we call your Morning Energizing Rituals. Begin your day by lying back down (if you're not lying down already) and giving yourself an invigorating Chi Belly Massage. Work out all your sore spots and body kinks. After that, proceed directly to your Morning Breathing Practice. Then sit on the edge of the bed and give yourself your morning Chi Body Massage. As you do so, cultivate a smile of gratitude for the many things you are doing to improve the fundamental conditions of your life—and for the many moments of *joie de vivre* that await you this week!

Fresh Start Question 7

Now that you have re-established your chi connection, you will begin this week of *joie de vivre* by answering the simplest, most important life question possible.

What brings me joy?

You'll need a pen, so please get one now and then sit down and make yourself comfortable. Take all the time you need to reflect before answering—or better yet, use your writing to arrive at your answer. Go ahead, begin to write out your search for the important answer to this question. Let the deeper truths of the spirit stream down your arm, through your hand, and onto the page. This should be your heart's response, not your mind's. Allow yourself that greatest of gifts: complete honesty.

You are after those simple, everyday pleasures that instill in you a sense of being alive, that bring you joy. Pure unfiltered joy—first time, second time, every time. What are those things for you, my friend? An evening's walk on the beach, in the country, through bustling city streets? Is it time alone with your dog, or is it the company of close friends? Is it dancing, a meal in a favorite restaurant? Browsing in a bookstore, going to a movie, a play, a concert? Whatever it is, write it down if it brings joy into your life. Now think of another, and another. Write them down, write them all down—the more the merrier! Are you finished? Wonderful. If you think of any more during the day, add them to your list tonight.

Now the follow-up questions: *When was the last time you did this?* and *When will you do it again?* If your answer to that last question isn't *this week,* ask yourself this: *What is stopping you from receiving the gift of joy in your life?* Remember, awareness follows change.

Four Ways to Awaken Dormant Curiosity

Are you curious about this activity? Good, that's one way!

Curiosity is a habit you have to cultivate: it's as simple as that. At first you might have none of it at all, but slowly, by using this activity's techniques, your curiosity will begin to loosen, to open, and finally to blossom. The more new things you learn, the more curious you will become. Curiosity is about the new, about engineering your life so that you begin to constantly encounter *the new*. That said, this first exercise is absolutely simple. Today, open at least one conversation with the phrase, *I'm just curious . . .* and then fill in the blank. Fill it in with something you've always wanted to know about the person you are speaking to, but have never bothered to ask. Perhaps it concerns their past, their favorite things, their accent, their clothes, an item on their desk, what they do on the weekend. It doesn't matter, whatever it is you are even remotely curious about, ask!

This question is simple, yet notice what happens once you've posed it, notice the response, notice the shift. Be alert for a change in the energy of the conversation, in the way this person responds, and in the exchanges that follow. You will probably become much more interested in this person. Did you perhaps consider this person stiff, rather dull, maybe hardly worth speaking to? Be prepared for all this to change!

Your question, your expression of interest, sends a powerful message of acceptance, of desire to know. This changes everything in the chemistry between people. Follow this exercise by thinking about what you learned as a result of your question. Ask yourself, why does this person think or act as they do? Ask yourself why they answered as they did. What was at the root of that response? Continue your journey of exploration regarding this person, with interest, with openness, but without a shred of judgment. Simply reflect upon what you now know, what you have just found out. Do this without reference to yourself: disregard the person's role in your life for a moment. Try to understand this person on their own terms, within their own frame of reference.

This exercise, so simple, so easy to accomplish, can start something quite wonderful, especially if lately you've begun to lose your curiosity about others, or if you never really had much to begin with! People are quite amazing if only you open up to them, see them as themselves. The "simplest" person, the waitress who serves you lunch, the cleaning staff at your workplace, the bartender. You never know what experiences they have had, what strange or wise or peculiar wisdoms they may possess. You never know about any of these things until you ask. If you engage in this activity regularly, you will begin to change the very nature of your responses to others and to the world. Don't underestimate it: it is very powerful. Discovering others in a nonjudgmental way is a profound practice. While judgment suppresses curiosity and imposes limits on our knowledge of others, openness and nonjudgmental curiosity about others expands and amplifies our knowledge, further stimulates our interest. Ignore what you think, for a change! It's not always that interesting or important, is it? How about considering what other people think! Now that might be really interesting!

The final thing I'd like you to try today is to select an opposing point of view and consider it carefully. Name a topic on which you have a clear opinion: it can be personal, political, anything. Now consider the position that is opposite or substantively different from your own. You might automatically wonder, how could anyone possibly believe this? But can it be that everyone with this viewpoint is a complete fool? Nonsense! (Or, if it is, you need to choose another issue.) Surely people have particular reasons for thinking as they do. Is it culture, religion, life experience? It has to be something, so spend some time figuring out what. Arrive at an accurate understanding of the set of experiences and circumstances that have led a person, or even a whole group of people, to see things in this particular way. This is an excellent practice for cultivating tolerance. While it does not require that you change your mind about something, it does require that you change your mind about some person. And this, dear reader, is one of the most challenging and life-rewarding changes possible. For that reason alone, try it! Challenge yourself today for the growth and wisdom it will bring you tomorrow!

My final request of you this morning is that you travel a new route to work today, or to wherever it is you are going. As you do so, take the time to notice the new things that come your way, the new people you encounter. Discovering the new is the best possible way to rekindle your curiosity and get out of the rut of the old, the ordinary, *the same old, same old.* Change your path and you change your day!

May your day be filled with new discovery and change!

Day №1   Evening

How did it go for you today? How was that conversation you started wtih the words *I'm just curious*? Surely you learned something you didn't know before. If it was something you didn't really need to know, don't give up—keep trying! I do hope your day was somehow new, somehow different, dear reader. Awakening your curiosity is such a vital part of awakening your spirit—don't you dare give up on it! Let's start with this evening's exercises:

1. Evening Cleansing Rituals: Wrist Shake, Arm Swing, Spinal Cord Breathing

2. 3Cs Meditation Practice

3. Reflection: The Experience of the Day

4. The Screening Room

Evening Cleansing Rituals

WRIST SHAKE, ARM SWING, SPINAL CORD BREATHING

You know these three rituals very well by now. Let's call them your Evening Cleansing Rituals from now on. Let them dissolve away the stresses and tensions of your day, this evening and every evening. If you've forgotten any of the practices in this set, refer back to the previous chapter to refresh your memory.

The 3Cs Meditation Practice

Now that you have released the negative energies stored in your body, sit down in your living room and finish the job by addressing your mind's desire for release. With your body-based and your mind-based clearing practices you should now be able to effectively rebalance yourself after a long day. This practice constitutes an act of loving kindness to yourself, so take a moment to appreciate the wonderful results of your new life conditioning, your ability to bring about balance in both mind and body. Be with yourself now, and say "calm, centered, connected." This simple practice brings you the peace and tranquility your mind naturally seeks. Provide it now, provide it tomorrow, provide it every evening for the rest of your life. *Calm, centered, connected.*

Reflection: The Experience of the Day

Did you enjoy your curiosity today? Did it come naturally? Perhaps you had to pretend, force it some. That's okay: that's often how things go at first—and that will change, as you know. If you didn't have to fake it, if you did summon some genuine curiosity, count it a blessing that you possess one of life's great gifts!

What other connections did you make today? On your new route, did you see new people, a building or a natural feature you don't usually see? Reflect on that experience, then: another blessing the day gave. Or perhaps you were able to see the world from another's perspective today. This ability is yet another gift, another small blessing in your life. Think some more about this now. Be glad for the day you had, whatever it was, however small its blessings. Cultivate just a little thankfulness now. Be with yourself for a moment and acknowledge any small joy or success you experienced today. Believe that tomorrow will bring with it its own particular joys as well. By paying close attention you will come to see each day as discrete, each day particular, each day unique. Be grateful for this.

The Screening Room

How are you doing in your practice of self-hypnosis? By now you should be beginning to sense a tangible transformation, the possibility of arriving at your desired vision. The seeds of new belief will, by now, be starting to germinate, becoming more concrete each day. The more visits to the Screening Room, the more power and clarity you will be giving your vision for change.

Stay acutely sensitive to signs of your awakening vision this week! Look for small changes in small places. Study carefully the life events you might have overlooked earlier. Are these the beginnings of change? Meditate upon this possibility. Recognize any and all indications of change, no matter their size! Perhaps these signs are only thoughts, only brief glimpses of new possibilities in your life. Acknowledge them! Know that such fragments are part of an emerging whole. Begin to assemble them!

Remember, dear reader, the Screening Room can be used for any desired change, anything you would like to actualize—just be sure you visualize any such desired change in explicit, concrete detail. Did I tell you that hypnosis is a very old practice? In fact, some ancient Greeks used it before going to sleep. Use it now, then sleep!

Bonne nuit, dear friend!

Day №2 Morning

Bonjour! By now you might be noticing the very real benefits of your morning chi sessions. Why are these so important to the start of your day? During the night your chi becomes dormant, goes to sleep as you do. A vigorous chi-based workout each morning helps you awaken and revitalize your body's energies to ensure success in your day. So let's get started:

1. Morning Energizing Rituals

2. The Diamond in the Heart Meditation

3. Three Ways to Connect to Yourself

4. Three Ways to Connect to Others

Morning Energizing Rituals

Chi Belly Massage, Morning Breathing Practice, Chi Body Massage: If they are not already, these morning rituals will become a way of life.

The Diamond in the Heart: A Meditation
TO BE LOVING TO YOURSELF

Prepare yourself with the 3Cs. Sit comfortably. Breathe deeply.

Put your hand to your heart. Listen to your heart beating its life song. Visualize a sparkling light within your body. When you exhale, know that with your breath you are creating a sacred space around you. When you inhale, know that you are absorbing into your body the sacred breath of life.

Continue to focus on the breath: *out*—creating the space your mind and spirit need; *in*—the golden light of oxygen rejuvenating your body. Notice, in time, the slackening of your breath. Notice that it is slowing,

slowing, taking you closer to your heart. Imagine the breath now filling your heart. Imagine that this light that now fills your heart is becoming radiant and white. Smile and admire the radiant light at the center of your heart. Look closely now and see the brilliant diamond at the center of this light. The diamond is you—all of it is you—the perfect beauty of you. Feel the pure, sparkling light of this idea, of this reality, as it warms your heart. Focus your attention on this radiant warmth. You are pure light, love, and kindness. You know this, don't you?

Think to yourself:

I embrace life with love and with honesty.
I am important.
My life counts.

Three Ways to Connect to Yourself

Now is the time to connect to yourself through the spirit. Now is the time to forget the job, the relationships, the responsibilities, the things. Now is the time for yourself. Take this time. Take it now; you have forever.

How will you know you are connected to the spirit? You will know when your life is guided mostly by that which is not visible. While you will always be aware of the material, of the physical, you will know you are connected to the spirit when you hear and trust and feel the guidance of your gentle voice of intuition. You will know it when you begin to regain your passion and your enthusiasm, when you believe every day is filled with the possibility of joy and success, when you no longer focus your energy and attention on what you want and need, but on what forwards you to your highest good and purpose. You will know it when your life becomes an adventure, when you actively seek out new connections to new people, when you find yourself being generous to them, when you feel the pulse and wave of empathy and loving kindness for others. You will know it when you rediscover your life purpose, your mission on the planet, when you become creative once more, when your imagination returns and is joined by the courage to look clearly at yourself and others. You will know you are connected to the spirit when you begin to see a transformation in your beliefs and attitudes and when you begin to feel the empowerment of positive outcomes.

Here now are three ways to enhance your connection to the spirit, allowing it active guidance in your life:

1. Create a sacred space in your home.

2. Listen to music that soothes your soul.

3. Dance to a rhythm that awakens the spirit of the body.

1. CREATE A SACRED SPACE

I told Elisabeth, one of my clients, to start collecting all the objects that had great meaning in her life: objects that lifted her up, that reminded her of her core values. Truly sacred objects are the first things one would fight for, the last things one would ever give up. Elisabeth selected eight objects: among them were a picture of herself as a young child with her mother and father, a high school photograph of her basketball team, a single earring that had belonged to her great-grandmother, a book of poems by a poet who had particular importance in her youth, and a picture of herself in her twenties when she was feeling particularly carefree. She placed these objects on a stand in her hallway so she could see them on her way to the bedroom. She noticed herself beginning to slow down more in her movements to and from this room. Each time she passed by, she took the time to glance at one or two of her sacred objects. This had the effect of slowing her thought processes down as well. By glancing down at that table, she was reminded of her life direction, reminded that her preoccupations of the moment were mere trifles. As you put together your own collection, I urge you to look in the nooks and crannies of your life, the boxes stowed in that storage area, basement, or garage. Strangely enough, we often put our most sacred objects into storage! If you can, find objects that give off an almost magnetic resonance, those things that fill you with joy when you simply glance at them. Take your time and enjoy your journey to the sacred!

Once you have a collection of objects from the "museum of self," find a special, visible place for them: some area that you will see at least once a day. Take the time to prepare and care for your altar. Buy some flowers with which to adorn it. Take all the time you need—your altar's value will grow with the time and energy you invest in it.

2. LISTEN TO MUSIC THAT SOOTHES YOUR SOUL

Music is the gateway to the spirit! It lets you bypass the preoccupations of the surface mind and penetrate deep into the soul, into the core of your being. You know this, of course, but perhaps you haven't ever considered the power of music as a therapeutic practice. I should like you to try it this week. Your musical choices are up to you, but make sure they move you deeply, make sure they have the power to uplift your spirit and soul. Maybe it's Stravinsky's *Firebird Suite,* or Patti LaBelle or the Beatles . . . or Richard Strauss, Frank Sinatra, Charles Aznavour, or maybe Bulgarian throat singing. Whatever your musical bliss, follow it to that deeper place. If it has lyrics, make sure they are positive. You may want to save the Rolling Stones' "Paint It Black" for a different practice!

Another powerful form of music therapy is chant. Chanting has been used for centuries to create positive, healing vibrational energy. One of my Chi Gong masters taught me a chant that I adore: take a deep in-breath, and as you slowly exhale, chant A-O-A (ah-oh-ah). Repeat five to nine times and enjoy the feeling of peace this chant instills, the resonance in your face, neck, and chest. Such vibrations reintegrate your mind and body and transport you almost immediately to a deeper, more spiritual place.

3. DANCE TO A RHYTHM THAT AWAKENS THE SPIRIT OF THE BODY

This is my favorite practice—I hope you will find it beneficial too!

The first time I engaged in dance therapy was during a workshop with the teacher and healer Gabriella Roth, the amazing author of *Sweat Your Prayers*. Roth believes that the various rhythms of music, combined with spontaneous body movements, lead the body to release its blockages and let its core energies emerge. Her technique calls for closed eyes—this allows the body absolute primacy. No choreography needed here. Just let your body find its own expression, and with your eyes closed you won't be self-conscious. This is a particularly useful exercise for people who are disconnected from their feelings: it awakens dormant emotions at the cellular level and, in the process, arouses the sleeping spirit within.

Three Ways to Connect to Others

Connecting to others is an essential part of the human experience: it allows the heart and the spirit the company of its fellows. Life without deep interaction with others is a solitary affair, is it not? The spirit needs and wants to express itself to its fellow spirits and fellow souls. We are not talking about everyday exchanges, but ones where affinities are shared, experiences and reflections communicated.

Let me remind you of some of the simplest, most basic channels for connecting to others: the smile, the compliment, and the acknowledgment.

1. THE POWER OF A SMILE

Sheila, a client of mine, was a power woman, successful, brilliant, the head of a major public relations firm. The magnitude of her responsibilities made her a serious woman—too serious, actually. Others perceived her as domineering, intimidating, even angry. She wasn't; she was simply deeply committed to fulfilling her many responsibilities. But with a demeanor as serious as hers, Sheila was having all sorts of problems professionally. Her employees feared her and kept their distance. Sheila grew isolated and, eventually, sad. She came to me at her wit's end, unable to see how the weight of her duties had made her into a boss nobody wanted anything to do with.

I suggested that she work on her smile. I'll never forget the look she gave me—as if I was completely cracked! I persisted, of course, telling her that when she practiced her smile, she was to imagine a beam of golden light linking her to her receiver's heart. Sheila didn't know what to make of that suggestion, but desperate for a solution, she resolved to give it a try. A week later, she called me to describe her new success—employees now flooded her office, they couldn't do enough for her, they asked for her advice on their projects. All these results from a simple smile. She still couldn't quite believe it!

It has been said that one is never fully dressed until one wears a smile: what a lovely thought! The smile is a picture of the heart, a genuine smile a blessing to both giver and receiver. A smile removes all traces of anger from within, dissolves all anger in the other. Is there any simpler joy than to be on the receiving end of a bighearted smile? It's pure magic, is it not? The best possible way to share one's joy of being in the world is to simply smile: consider your smile as yet another gift of immeasurable value (and free in the giving). Did you know it takes only seven muscles to generate a smile—and fifty muscles to frown! Give out some smiles today and enjoy the happiness of making others happy!

2. THE POWER OF A COMPLIMENT

You have been on the receiving end of a great compliment or two in your life, have you not? How did you feel? Did you feel a rush of joy throughout your body? Did it change your mood completely? I bet it did. How can a single compliment have such a powerful effect: did you ever wonder that? It's simple, isn't it? A compliment is the ultimate expression of appreciation and acceptance. It simply warms the heart.

We have such power to make others happy. Expressing some curiosity about them, flashing them a smile, giving them the splendid gift of a compliment—we can change another's day completely. Marvelous, isn't it? So listen, the next time you meet someone new or someone you haven't seen in a while, find something positive to say early in the conversation. Try to be original and genuine, of course—avoid those tired old compliments. Validate something about the other person: a viewpoint they expressed, a valuable perspective they offered, something they did well. Then notice what happens. Most likely, the person will warm to you immediately, and may even bless you with a return compliment. By the end of the encounter, the world will have two more smiling people on its hands—all for the price of a generous statement or two.

Enjoy the feeling of giving a compliment; enjoy the pleasure you give another. Do it again later in the day—giving compliments is addictive! When you have mastered the spontaneous compliment, work on throwing in a warm, genuine smile; learn to look clearly into another's eyes as you tell them they are wonderful. They will love you for it—and you will love yourself for doing it. (Don't let that head swell too much, however—remember, *humility* is the key to *joie de vivre* and human happiness.)

3. THE POWER OF ACKNOWLEDGMENT

I'm sure you have had the experience, during a conversation, of someone abruptly changing the topic without so much as a transition or a nod in your direction. Or perhaps nothing you said seemed to register; it was simply ignored—as if you weren't there at all. Once you finished what you were saying, the other person promptly picked up where they had left off, as if you hadn't ever opened your mouth. Perhaps you have even done this to others once or twice—we have to be honest now, right?.

Do you remember how you felt as a result of this experience? Probably at least a bit irritated, maybe even angry. To be ignored, to be dismissed is a terrible feeling. People need and deserve to have their views acknowledged. This is a basic human right, actually. Acknowledgment shows appreciation of another being, and it can fundamentally change relationships. This may strike you as simple stuff, but there is simply not enough of it in the world, is there? In your conversations this week, practice the power of acknowledgment and see how it can transform your encounters. Acknowledging does not mean agreeing with everything that is said—it means expressing respect for another's views, opinions, and, ultimately, existence. If you would like to explore this topic, I highly recommend Judith W. Umlas' book *The Power of Acknowledgment*. Umlas outlines the seven fundamental principles of acknowledgment, explaining how, when properly applied, they repair the world by transforming its energy and strengthening its spirit.

The next time you are in the company of a friend, colleague, or even a stranger, make them feel special by acknowledging them. And, if you have the appropriate moment, say *I believe in you*. This may be the greatest acknowledgment possible. Lifelong relationships are founded upon this simple article of faith expressed to another.

Day № 2   Evening

Bonsoir, and how was your day? Did you make any new or stronger connections with others today? If this approach feels new to you, give yourself some time to get it right! All that is needed is the courage to keep trying. The opportunities for a smile, a compliment, an expression of curiosity or acknowledgment are renewed with each new day. This evening's activities are:

1. Evening Cleansing Rituals
2. Finger Therapy
3. The Garden of the Heart Meditation
4. Victory Count

Evening Cleansing Rituals

Wrist Shake, Arm Swing, Spinal Breathing: it's time to let go of the day, move your body, make some silly sounds, and clear yourself of your accumulated negative energies. The more negative energy you release, the better your evening will be.

Finger Therapy

Sit comfortably, play some calming music, and use those fingers to release the emotions of the day.

The Garden of the Heart Meditation
TO CULTIVATE LOVE FOR THE SELF

For this meditation, you need a vase of flowers—if you keep flowers in your sacred place, use those. Ideally, you will seat yourself in front of your personal altar, but if you can't manage this, simply place the vase directly in front of you where you are sitting.

Make yourself comfortable and begin with the 3Cs to calm and clear your head. Once you are clear, open your eyes and stare at the flowers. Concentrate your full attention on one particular flower, your favorite of the bunch. See this flower now. Breathe in its scent, feel its beauty in your heart. Imagine that this flower belongs to your heart, to the garden of your heart. In this garden, everything is perfect, and the way you like it to be. Once you have meditated upon this thought for a moment, take the flower in your hands and place it over your heart. As you hold the flower, breathe in to that garden. Now imagine planting this flower in the center of your heart. Nurture it with a loving smile. Right now and from now on, you are the gardener of your heart. Take pride in cultivating your garden. Shine on it the love it needs to grow. Be witness to the beauty of your heart's blossoming joy.

Victory Count

I know you had some victories today. What with your complimenting and smiling and acknowledging and so on, you must have been really something—I wish I'd been there! Now it is time to write your victories down. You are moving forward to your vision of change—keep score by recording the successes you are enjoying. You are a brave warrior; chronicle your victories! Make it epic. When you are finished, give yourself a resounding *I Can, I Do, I Will*. Victory is yours!

Sleep well, fellow warrior.

Day №3   Morning

Bonjour, dear friend. Laughter and fun are on the morning menu—you're ready for these, I trust? Here's what we'll do.

1. Morning Energizing Rituals

2. Fresh Start Question 8

3. A Few Ways to Laugh

4. Assignment: Joke of the Day

Morning Energizing Rituals

You are probably now experiencing much more energy in your life as a result of these daily chi rituals. They really are the best possible way to get the day going. All right then, onward and upward!

Fresh Start Question 8

Pick up a pen and answer this question:

In what concrete ways can I be more loving to myself?

Please take all the time you need. Take three deep breaths to clear the necessary inner space—then let the pen do the writing. Allow your arm and hand to simply transmit the energy of words from the subconscious to the conscious mind and onto the page.

I recall a client of mine who simply could not answer this question. Try as she might, the pen refused to move; the answer remained within. The problem? Debbie did not know what it meant to be loving—at least to herself. I finally suggested she start by thinking about how she treated her two children, and imagining treating herself in the same way. She began to cry. Why? At that moment she came to the sudden recognition that she had never treated herself the way she always treated the ones she loved. All her life, Debbie had put herself last—consequently, she had never taken the time to love herself even one little bit—she had never quite gotten around to loving herself! After her startling epiphany, she began to find some time for herself at last: she enrolled in some art classes, treated herself to a massage now and again, began to express her needs to her family, eventually even found herself capable of asking for outside help. While your predicament may not be just like Debbie's, you probably take far too few small, loving actions toward yourself. Come up with a list now and follow through with some of these loving acts this week. Composing this list is, in fact, a loving act in itself. So begin to show the love now, why don't you? *Joie de vivre* begins in loving yourself, don't you know!

A Few Ways to Laugh

A good laugh cures all! Laughter has been known to literally reverse serious disease. It stimulates the immune system and floods the body with endorphins and other essential biochemicals.

Humor also gives us perspective, lets us detach and see life from a different perspective—one that is often supremely comical! Laughter undercuts the seriousness of crisis, letting us suddenly see it in perspective. And seeing it so, we solve it, often by dissolving it with laughter. Absurdity is a good beginning here. Think of a problem, a dilemma that you may be experiencing these days. Now inflate it. Make the characters comical by exaggerating one or two of their defining features. Imagine all those involved, including yourself, to be two-dimensional cartoon figures. This can be a lot of fun, once you get the hang of it.

When I first came to New York City I was giggling almost constantly. Why? Because so many people I saw on the street resembled the animated characters in American cartoons. I came to see that these fictional characters weren't created out of thin air: they were simply exaggerations of ordinary people. New Yorkers struck me as so completely over-the-top that it was all too easy to see them as cartoons. I laughed till I cried!

Once you have made animated characters of the people in your current life drama, develop the plotline. How will things turn out? Will Popeye get to his tin of spinach, or will Brutus tie those knots so tight that Olive Oyl is finally doomed? You'll have to find parallels between these silly storylines and your real-life crises, but this may be easier than you think! A little creativity and imagination and you'll be laughing yourself through your crisis! Give yourself some time to develop your ability to turn life into art, or at least into cartoons—you'll be glad you did!

I always laugh when I think of my swimming-pool crisis. One day I decided to go for a swim to relax before an important meeting with a prospective corporate client. At the pool I put on my purple hairband and dove in. Well, it turned out that the water was so over-chlorinated that day that it bleached the dye out of my hairband, transferring it perfectly to my hair, which is quite blond. When I emerged from the pool into the dressing room, I almost died. I looked like something out of Barnum and Bailey! I scrubbed and scoured my head until it was numb, but the wide purple stripe clung stubbornly to my hair. With a crucial meeting in just over an hour, I knew I was doomed.

As I stood on the subway headed downtown, the absurdity of my situation suddenly dawned on me. I began to laugh out loud. Nearby, I saw a young man in punk regalia—black leather jacket, torn jeans, nose ring, the works—exchange smiles with a woman he must have figured to be a middle-aged punk rocker. Inspiration! That would be my persona: an aging punk rock chick who refused to acknowledge the march of time. I had planned to buy a hat to wear for the meeting, but I was so entranced by my new identity that I chucked that idea.

Soon after, I strode confidently into the boardroom and faced a gallery of incredulous executives. I sat down and gave the moment the time it needed. Then I told my story, apparently with such *joie de vivre* that I was immediately awarded the contract. As one executive put it, the person who could so forthrightly tell a story at her own expense was the person they wanted to conduct their employee wellness training.

Later that night, I put on jeans and a leather jacket and my husband and I celebrated my victory by dropping by the East Village punk scene. Unbelievably, while my husband stepped away to make a phone call, the very same guy who had inspired me on the subway that morning came by to chat me up! Though I didn't give him the chat he was looking for, I did thank him for his inspiration. Out of disaster came success—all it took was a comical view!

The secret to using humor to transcend life's minor tragedies is to fully visualize them as comedies. The more vivid and specific the comedy, the more it will transform your experience or, to put it simply, the harder you'll laugh! Laughter has been such a blessing in my life that I even summon it in the absence of crisis. When I do the skull-tapping part of my chi-based morning workout (just like you, my friend!), I sometimes picture my brain cells as miniature creatures responding to the taps with somersaults, cartwheels, and traditional Irish dancing. Absolutely silly, of course, but it gets me laughing every time. This is exactly the kind of silliness the day deserves, is it not! At other times I look at Sophie, my little Maltese, and imagine her as a Fu Manchu sage with long white sideburns, telling me the many wisdoms she has acquired in her long life. This gets me going every time—and Sophie enjoys it too!

If you are naturally humorous, give credit to your parents or whatever influence got you going down the comical path. I credit my mother for her exquisite sense of humor and for showing me time and time again how humor can be life's saving grace. She is the funniest person I have ever met—bar none. Even today, in her seventies, she gets me going to the point where I have to beg for her to stop. Together, we laugh so hard that when we are in a public space we are often treated to concerned glances—I'm sure there are some who consider us absolutely cracked. Of course, this only makes us laugh even harder!

Joke of the Day: An Assignment

Find a joke you like and learn it by heart. Tell it to at least three people today. Make them laugh—and be sure you laugh with them. Later in the day, create a joke out of a serious event you witnessed, or of which you were a part.

Tip of the Day

KEEP IT LIGHT

Stop taking yourself so seriously. That's an order! When you find yourself descending into irredeemable seriousness, pull yourself up! Find something funny to enjoy. Cultivate laughter and you'll cultivate *joie de vivre*.

Day №3 Evening

Bonsoir, dear reader! I hope you had a few good laughs today. How did that joke go? Were you able to use it to create some good cheer? Did this help you connect with others? I hope so. I also hope you had the wonderful experience of melting your daily stress away by the dissolving power of laughter—could anything be better?

Continue this new practice all this week and into the next and the next. With time, humor becomes habit, a habit you will be unwilling to break. You may even find yourself liking yourself more! It's okay, you can laugh aloud several times a day and still live up to your responsibilities—only you'll find yourself doing a much better job with them. Now let's get started.

1. Evening Cleansing Rituals

2. 3Cs Meditation Practice

3. Golden Chalice Meditation

4. Garden of the Heart Meditation, with a hand as an anchor

Evening Cleansing Rituals

I'm sure you know what you're up to with these now! Enjoy!

The 3Cs Meditation Practice

Follow your practice of the cleansing rituals with the 3Cs and enjoy an absolutely stress-free evening—these two are an unbeatable combination.

The Golden Chalice Meditation
TO CULTIVATE ABUNDANCE IN YOUR LIFE

I want you to imagine something that, if handed to you, you would accept instinctively, without so much as a thought. Imagine you are handed, for example, a sleeping baby, a cheerful puppy, a kitten, a warm blanket, a priceless antique crystal decanter. Whatever it is, make it something you would simply, unthinkingly accept. Meditate on the feeling you would experience with such an acceptance.

Now imagine you have been handed a golden chalice filled with a magical, healing, life-giving alchemical preparation. Take this goblet in your hands. Hold it there a moment in anticipation of its contents. When you have recognized the need for such power in your life, tilt the chalice up to your lips and drink deeply of it. That's it, drink it all down. The elixir of life warms your throat and your belly on contact. This warmth spreads rapidly throughout your body, coursing through your limbs, up to your neck, face, and head.

Invite good things to come into your life now. Give yourself permission to accept their abundance, just as you accepted the contents of the chalice. Open yourself to a new wealth of positive thoughts, energy, people, and events. Breathe out deeply now, and as you do so, imagine that you are creating space for all these good things.

Every time you are offered a gift in life, know that you deserve it. As you learn to accept small things, you will learn to allow for larger things—money, love, spiritual growth, inner peace, your higher purpose. Be open, accept that these will come into your life because they are your due, because you fully deserve them. Take a moment now to enjoy this feeling of deserving.

Express gratitude to the universe for all you have, for all your many blessings. Remember, what you focus on expands. Focus on the positive and it will expand.

Think to yourself:

I choose to have a joyful life.
I give thanks for all I have.
I welcome further abundance into my life.

Every time you take a moment to appreciate what you already have, abundance will come into your life.

The Garden of the Heart Meditation, with a hand as an anchor

Last night you placed a flower over your heart and planted a garden to grow there. Tonight you will repeat this meditation, but with your hand instead of a flower. Look again at the flower and meditate upon its beauty and splendor. Once you have this feeling of reverence, recall the sensation of this flower against your heart. Take a moment to be with this experience. Then place your dominant hand over your heart—your hand is now this flower. Stay a moment there and summon the feeling of the garden of the heart.

At any time during your day when you feel a need to reconnect to your loving self again, place your hand over your heart and experience your beautiful garden of the heart. Follow this practice with three deep loving breaths and a smile of contentment. Be sure to take the time to meditate upon this joyful experience!

Day Nº4   Morning

Good morning—how did you sleep? Let's get started on this morning's exercises.

1. Morning Energizing Rituals

2. Three Ways to Show Compassion and Kindness

3. Mindful Warrior Walk

Morning Energizing Rituals

You know what to do. Enjoy!

Three Ways to Show Compassion and Kindness

Compassion is the keen awareness of the interdependence of all things.

THOMAS MERTON

Compassion is the ultimate and most meaningful embodiment of emotional maturity. It is through compassion that a person achieves the highest peak and deepest reach in his or her search for self-fulfillment.

ARTHUR JERSILD

Never apologize for showing feelings, when you do so you apologize for the truth

BENJAMIN DISRAELI

Today is your day to play the saint. Take your pick: (a) the Dalai Lama or (b) Mother Teresa. You think I'm kidding? I'm not! Even if it's the only such day of your entire life, today you are going to be holy, a paradigm of goodness and compassion. I promise you will have fun!

All right, you have your robes on, excellent! Here are your three sacred assignments:

1. SHOW KINDNESS TO THE MOST DIFFICULT PERSON IN YOUR LIFE TODAY

Don't go easy on yourself, now. I want you to choose someone you absolutely cannot stand! Be of service to this person. Help this person out in one way or another. Praise them. Acknowledge them—trust me, this will be very interesting.

Some sage or other said, "There are no difficult people, there are only different people." The Dalai Lama himself said that "the important thing is not to be right, but to be loving." Look, those people we find so difficult just think a little differently, that's all. Because they think differently, they say and do things we simply cannot understand. Thus we react. Our *reactions* create our difficulties. The trick to holiness here is to simply accept this person's difference without judgment, without any reaction whatsoever. "This person is different from me," that's all you have to say—and you'll be a saint. Carry on. Complete your acts of kindness and break through the barrier that separates you from them. In so doing, you will also break the pattern of your relationship to this person. Changing our approach changes everything. Other people are not "annoying," we become annoyed by them. You have the power to change everything. It's entirely in your own hands. All you have to do is get past your irritation, get past your reaction—and just accept this person as simply *different*. If you think it will help, consider the nature of the difference. Is it cultural, age- or gender-related, temperamental? A difference in emotional intelligence? Maybe they were just born that way—consider! And ask, "Does this person choose to be different explicitly to annoy or irritate me?" If your answer is yes, keep trying! If you are dealing with a supremely "annoying" person, one almost universally seen as difficult, you may need to take more drastic measures. Such people probably are, quite frankly, a little sick. No, really—I'm not being cruel here, only realistic. If you've got such a person on your hands, treat them as slightly sick, unwell, I mean. That helps, doesn't it? What, you would mistreat the sick? Come on, now. Have compassion for this person, who may have been mistreated in some way as a child, ending up with serious problems. Imagine this person as a dog who was mistreated as a puppy—such dogs have behavioral problems. They growl, they bite, they snarl. It's quite sad, actually. Such dogs, such people, are in constant pain. Of all beings, they are the most absolutely deserving of love and compassion. There, that should make this easier—and you thought sainthood was difficult! Difficult people are different, and sometimes as the result of tragic circumstances. They want love, as you do—chances are they need it twice as much. You have the power to make a difference in that person's life. Are you up to it? Are you ready to meet such a higher challenge? I bet you are. If you're up for it, give this person a hug. This may startle them, so take care in your approach and, above all, be sincere.

2. BE OF SERVICE TO ANOTHER TODAY

In Paris recently, my husband and I were plodding through a metro station with our two massive suitcases. We reached a staircase and before we knew it, a man had picked up one of the suitcases and begun to carry it up the steps. After a moment of alarm (too many years in New York, I suppose), we realized he was not making off with the bag, only helping us with it. It was a small act of kindness, but I still remember it now.

Perform such a service today. You'll be glad you did, and you'll have created one more grateful heart—the world could use a few more!

3. VOLUNTEER TO HELP SOMEONE TODAY

Do you know a child who needs a tutor? Is there an old man or woman in your neighborhood who could use some extra assistance? Volunteer your service to such a person. Give of yourself, give of your time. The smallest acts of kindness become magnified over time. They begin to change the world incrementally. You have it in your power to change another's life. There are no small acts of kindness—all kindnesses are immense.

The Mindful Warrior Walk

You may remember this exercise from last week. Try it again today, remembering to be absolutely mindful of your walking body. Be sure to make that connection between feet and earth, eyes and sky. As you focus on the simple act of walking, you will let go of your daily stresses and anxieties. In the absolute present, there is peace. Bring your attention to the present moment by bringing your consciousness to bear on the motion of your limbs and feet.

Day № 4   Evening

Bonsoir, dear reader. Did you enjoy being a saint today? Did you experiment with showing compassion and kindness? Remember, those choices are is available to you at any time. This evening's activities:

1. Evening Cleansing Rituals

2. 3Cs Meditation Practice

3. The Satellite Meditation

4. Reflection: Apply the Satellite in Your Life

Evening Cleansing Rituals

Okay, you're on your own now—you can do it by yourself. Cleanse that stress!

The 3Cs Meditation Practice

Calm, center, connect. Practice your 3Cs in preparation for the meditation that follows.

The Satellite Meditation: An Introduction

There are those in life with whom we have had such a difficult history that we simply prefer not to see them any more. Sadly, such people are often those with whom we have shared much. Perhaps that is why we no longer see them, because with such a shared past, the discord of the present can simply be too great to bear. But silence between two who have been close comes with a terrible price. Though we are not consciously aware of it, it plays emotional havoc on our subconscious minds, manifesting itself in other, seemingly unrelated, unhappinesses. It is impossible to know anything like absolute peace with one or more such severed relationships in our lives. Even if we don't notice it, the underlying psychological agitation disturbs us too much for us to ever arrive at contentment and tranquility.

Isn't it time to heal? You need peace, and so does the other. But to arrive finally at peace, something must shift. Since it is folly to expect the other to change by waiting for them to come around to your way of thinking, it's up to you to find a way past the impasse. If you suffer such severed relationships, seek guidance or counseling so you can find the strength and courage to heal yourself and the other. Begin this process with the following meditation.

The Satellite Meditation
TO RECONCILE ONESELF TO OTHERS

Imagine now that you are a satellite. As a satellite, you are both a receiver of energy and a transmitter of energy. The energy you send and receive travels around the globe. You are, in fact, an integral part of a much larger human energy transmission system. You are broadcasting at all times, day and night, whether you are aware of it or not. Tune in to your frequency now. Imagine that you are broadcasting pure loving kindness throughout the world.

First, send a transmission to one you love dearly. Visualize that face as you do so—this is how you direct your transmission. Now broadcast the same loving kindness to an acquaintance, someone you know but do not necessarily love. Again, direct it by concentrating on this person's face. Finally, think of one whom you once loved, but toward whom you now feel ambivalence or enmity because they have hurt or wronged you deeply. Take your time to do this, making sure it is kindness and goodwill you are transmitting. This person is, after all, worthy of kindness! This person too has suffered, is suffering now. Send this person compassion and loving kindness now. Take this moment to create the possibility of future love and harmony between you now.

Think to yourself:

I recognize that each is different.
I respect the difference of others; I respect their uniqueness.
Harmony, peace, and joy flow through me now.
I wish happiness, peace, and the blessings of life to all.

Cultivating loving kindness for others, especially those who have hurt us in some way, begins to clear the path toward reconciliation. This may be a most difficult challenge, but consider the price of failure. Trust that you will have the courage to accomplish this—know that your life can be utterly transformed through such reconciliations with others. Keep an open heart and an open mind. Believe, once again, that love is possible.

Reflection: Applying the Satellite Meditation in Your Life

Before you go to sleep tonight, reflect on the idea that you are a satellite, constantly sending and receiving emotional energies. If you can't quite come to believe this rationally, make it a possibility at least—simply be open to the idea. Smile at the idea that out of your mind-body radiates an energy that travels the planet, from Albuquerque to the Azores, from Nantucket to Normandy and beyond. Run with the idea that you can use this network to broadcast kindness to the rest of humanity. Send some love right now. Consider sending a broadcast to those places torn by war or famine or disease. Use the images of the evening newscast in your visualization. Send loving kindness to the faces you saw from the comfort of your living room. Go to sleep with your transmitter on. The most peaceful night's sleep to you now, dear reader.

Day №5   Morning

Bonjour! Today you will look at your own talents and passions—and you'll express your appreciation for the people who are blessings in your life. Here are the morning's activities:

1. Morning Energizing Rituals

2. Fresh Start Question 9

3. A Few Ways to Show Gratitude and Appreciation

Morning Energizing Rituals

You know the routine! Rejuvenate and invigorate.

Fresh Start Question 9

Take a pen and answer this question:

What are my talents and passions?

Take your time with this one. Access your deeper space with a few deep breaths, letting the answer come from that place within. Once again, use your hand and arm as the conduit for your buried truths. If the answers are not readily available, use writing to reflect on the page. In the meantime, let me tell you about my client Martha.

When I first met Martha, she was sixty years old. She had been successful in business, but wasn't quite clear what she wanted at this stage of her life. Other than her job, her only significant pastime was collecting "outside art." For many years she had been gathering work by artists who were completely outside of the artistic mainstream. Though she felt guilty for the money she spent on it, it was, as she put it, an "irresistible indulgence." During the course of my work with Martha, it became clear that her real passion in life was her unofficial vocation as an art collector. I presented this to her one day, and she was completely taken aback. What was obvious to me, what should have been obvious to anyone who knew Martha at all, was that collecting such art was her bliss. And she was the last person to acknowledge it. Once she came to accept that this work was more important to her than anything else in the world, it changed the conditions of her life entirely. She gave up her day job, threw herself into her passion, and emerged a much happier, much more successful person. Today she is one of the United States' foremost collectors of this highly specialized art. Martha's "indulgence" was her passion, practically her very reason for being. She needed only to see this herself before she could change, rebuilding her life around what she most loved to do.

All of us are born with such gifts, of course, but so few of us follow them. This is such a shame. How often do we slip dutifully into the track of expectations laid out for us by parents, spouses, peers? When we do this, we sacrifice not only our passions, but ourselves. What possibility for *joie de vivre* is there when we are most occupied with fulfilling responsibilities that were either imposed upon us, or perhaps were accepted under the duress of family, cultural, or economic pressures?

My own life, as planned by others around me, was to consist of education and then a successful marriage and motherhood in France. Luckily for me, I had my epiphany on the beach at fifteen. Unable to suppress my passion, I held on to my life's bliss despite the considerable pressures exerted against me. Eventually my mother's own passionate nature came to the aid of my own, and I traveled with her to America. How unlikely that I would have become a writer and teacher without this loving assistance and support!

Some people seem to know from a very young age what they want. Others discover it later through trial and error. How it happens doesn't matter: what matters is that once discovered, one's passion must be honored. The costs of dishonoring passion can be enormous. Of course many of us do have unavoidable responsibilities and duties. That's okay,

I'm not suggesting you dump your spouse, your job, and your children to take up residence in a garret. Start small. Carve out a little space for your passions and eventually you will find your life opening to allow you greater and greater investment in this area. This simply happens over time. But you must take the first step—everything depends on this. My own career as a teacher had its humble beginnings in the halls of the UN, as a tour guide. It was there that I discovered the joy I felt in helping others to their own discoveries.

Ask yourself: Who am I? Am I a teacher? An organizer or promoter? An artist? One who works with people? A healer? A communicator? One of my clients is a financial advisor by weekday, and a language teacher to underprivileged children in the evenings and on weekends. She loves both, would give up neither. It is possible to negotiate between obligations and passions, you know! Begin now, dear reader.

A Few Ways to Show Gratitude and Appreciation

There is a lovely little anecdote about a Zen master named Sono. Hundreds came to seek the enlightened one's advice, many traveling miles of difficult terrain to do so. But regardless of the length of their journeys, the desperateness of their circumstances, Sono's advice was always the same for one and for all. Whether the story was long and involved or short and simple, Sono listened to the seeker patiently and quietly. When it was completed, he gave the supplicant the only words he or she should ever utter in response to any life event or circumstance: *I am thankful for everything. I have no complaint whatsoever.*

Sono's advice is a challenge to us, of course. How many days in your life have you had no complaint? The enlightened know what we sometimes dimly perceive: whatever we give our attention to grows and becomes energized. Whatever we focus on expands. This is the simple law of the universe—and though we seem to know it to be true, how many of us practice it by choosing to feed and magnify the positive in our lives? We are back to our good wolf here, dear friend. Will we feed the one who would be grateful, or will we feed the one who is drawn to complaint, to an obsessive concern with what it does not possess?

Have you ever seen a calendar of the many official recognition days observed in the United States? Such a good idea, and quite an impressive list. The opportunities for official recognition very nearly fill every day of the year. We have Dental Assistants Recognition Week, Get to Know Your Customers Day, Thank a Mailman Day, Intravenous Nurse Day, Clean Out Your Computer Day, National Salesperson Day, Golfers Day, National Auctioneers Day, Beauticians Day, Take Your Webmaster to Lunch Day, Insurance Awareness Day, Be Kind to Editors and Writers Month, System Administrator Appreciation Day, Newspaper Carrier Day, International Women's E-Commerce Awareness Day, National Custodial Workers Day, Farmers Day. The list goes on.

The basic impulse here is wonderful, of course. It's true that we have many, many people in our lives to be thankful for. But just a thought here: perhaps before recognizing the mailman, the paperboy, and the webmaster, we might begin a little closer to home. How about recognizing the people who kindly find it in their hearts to love us! Aren't these the people who are often the most taken for granted? Perhaps we should designate official recognition days for those who love us well. National Express Some Affection for Your Spouse Day, Thank Your Best Friend Week, Sisters Day, Brothers Day. Or, perhaps we can learn to recognize those who dearly love and support us without the help of a desk calendar! Shouldn't you make a list of those who wish you happiness and success? Shouldn't you begin to be grateful to these human treasures? Compile your list now, and once you have it, take a moment to cultivate gratefulness for these human blessings in your life. Then, begin to express it! Trust that such expression will open your heart. It will. Trust also that such acknowledgment will not go unnoticed by the universe—what we focus on expands: expand your field of thankfulness and you will be blessed with more to be thankful for.

Okay, take a moment now to be thankful for this day—come on, you can do it. Yes, it seems, well, a little granola, but come on, it will do you good! Have you ever had the thought that there will come a day that you *won't* be a part of? We all hope this day is many, many days away, but a day will come when you won't be irritatedly awoken by your alarm clock. Okay, with that thought in mind you are probably ready to cultivate some gratitude that today you did, in fact, wake up, that this morning your slumber did not stretch out into eternity.

Now I'd like you to identify three people in your life who you would like receive the recognition and blessing of your gratitude. Put that cell phone gadget to some good use today. Call them and let them know that you love them and that you appreciate the blessing of having them in your life. Make plans to see them soon.

Finally, I'd like you to commit to a temporary ceasefire in your judgment of others—until midnight tonight, at the very least. See if you can get through one day without a single criticism, a single complaint about any other living being. Try out Sono's advice. Repeat after me: *I am thankful for everything. I have no complaint whatsoever.* Designate today as Personal Nonjudgment of Others Day! Make tomorrow Recognition, Acknowledgment, and Praise of Others Day. Now you're getting the idea. Don't take this mission lightly, however. Old habits die hard! But you can do this, and you will be breaking old patterns and establishing more positive conditioning.

Have a wonderful day today. Know that I have designated it Edwige's Appreciation of Her Readers Day. Make it your best day ever—this is in your power now. Your life is in your own hands!

Day №5 Evening

How was your Personal Nonjudgment of Others Day? I hope you didn't find it too big a challenge. There is, of course, great benefit in treating other people well. Cultivating kindness feels good, doesn't it? As a feeling in the body, kindness is second only to laughter for the pleasure it gives. The choice is yours: let your body be eaten away by the acidic biochemical components underlying your feelings of irritation, frustration, and judgment . . . or have your body caressed, cleansed, and enervated by the life-sustaining biochemicals that underlie kindness, gratitude, and appreciation. Being good feels good, doesn't it! Let's proceed.

1. Evening Cleansing Rituals

2. Sound Therapy: The Six Healing Sounds

3. Mindful Eating with Appreciation

4. Victory Count

Evening Cleansing Rituals

Go to it now and enjoy the benefits of a peaceful, calm evening.

Sound Therapy: Practicing the Six Healing sounds

You have cleansed yourself of the negative emotions of the day? Wonderful! Now you are ready to engage the healing power of sound to complete your evening's cleanse. If you've forgotten how to make your healing sounds, review the instructions in the previous chapter.

Mindful Eating with Appreciation

How's the eating going these days? I hope that you are still using the Five Bites technique. As simple as it is, this practice can have significant results. I have seen many clients shed ten, fifteen, even twenty pounds.

At your evening meal, take time to appreciate not only the food that blesses your table, but also the fact that eating supplies your body with energy. Recognize and revere the body by feeding it healthful, wholesome food tonight. Develop awareness of your emotional state as you prepare and eat your food: are you eating because your body needs food? Or because you are stressed out, or perhaps bored, and eating is your only pleasure? Awareness of eating requires an awareness of our emotional states while we eat. Eat enough to fill your body's needs. Eat slowly enough to fully experience the many wonderful flavors of the blessing of food as it enters your mouth.

Victory Count

With each new day of your Fresh Start Promise, you experience newer, greater victories. Take credit now for all you have accomplished today. Give yourself that essential pat on the back. Acknowledge yourself for acknowledging others—go ahead, celebrate your victories!

Day №6 Morning

This morning: your basic morning rituals, a brand-new practice, and more mindful walking. Here's the plan:

1. Morning Energizing Rituals

2. Three Ways to Develop Intuition

3. Mindful Warrior Walk

Morning Energizing Rituals
All right, up and at 'em!

Three Ways to Develop Intuition
We all possess intuition, but few of us use it. We don't use it because we don't really trust it—let's face it, we live in a rational world where powers such as intuition are heavily discounted. But you are different, of course: you've purchased this book and are using it to change your life. You, at least, have something of an open mind, since you have already acted upon something very close to intuition. Now I would like you to act a little more!

What is intuition? Let's come to a common understanding of this human faculty before we continue. Intuition is a knowing that is pre-cognitive, pre-linguistic. It is the innate understanding of a truth or a correct action. It is immediate—it is not arrived at, it simply arrives. It comes as much from the body as the mind, which is why we also call it a gut feeling. Work with that, then: the gut never lies. It is visceral, since it comes from the viscera—literally, the gut.

Like a muscle, intuition gets stronger with use. Like a radio receiver, our sense of our own intuition requires fine tuning. Using this faculty requires both a broadcast ("Hello, this is your gut calling") and a reception ("What's up, gut?"). Bear in mind that as you begin to tune in to your intuition today, and in the days to come, you are likely to experience some interference and static. The messages you receive may be garbled, even incoherent. Intuition, when it is fine-tuned, is not enigmatic, it is crystal clear. It is digital. Give yourself some time to get better at listening and tuning in to your intuitive channels. If you are a very rational, logical type, you may have to search up and down the dial to pick up anything at all! Don't worry, with time it will come. Cultivate some trust. Be patient.

One of the many benefits of intuition is that it is a great aid in our relationships with others. Well-received intuition about another person can literally save us days, weeks, months in coming to understand them. In incredibly short bursts, your intuition sends you such a densely packed stream of information; you will possess almost everything you need to know about the other. But it may be like a compressed computer file; you may need time to decompress and process this information—perhaps even a few days. Take the time.

Intuition is also a phenomenal decision-making tool. Successful people often have an incredibly well developed intuitive system. Combining this with information and intellect, they are unstoppable—unless, of course, they tune out their intuition. Read a few accomplished people's autobiographies and you will see this time and again.

The key to using intuition in your decision making lies in your ability to distinguish between it and your intellect. These are two very different information processing systems, so confusing the two can be a disaster! If you trust your intuition absolutely, but mistake your intellect for your intuition, you can get yourself into some real difficulty. Placing as much trust in your intellect as your intuition is a serious mistake, because the intellect is far from infallible, astoundingly far. (It's ironic, then, that most of us place absolute faith in the intellect.)

About ten years ago, I lived in what must have been the smallest studio apartment in New York City—even Sophie, my little Maltese, complained. Every morning I took her for a much-needed walk around the block. Several weeks into the routine, I began to look at this one building in the middle of the block. There was nothing particularly notable about it, yet each day I found my eyes trained there again. After a month or more of this routine, I was actually fully mesmerized by that building. As I gazed at it one day I realized that it would be my next home. This made no rational sense at all, of course. It was a co-op building, cooperatively owned, and therefore offered absolutely no chance of my renting an apartment there. Not having an abiding confidence in human faculty of reason, however, I walked up and spoke with the doorman. He smiled, confirmed that the building was a co-op, and that seemed to be that. But, interestingly, I was not put off by this information. It just didn't seem to make sense, despite its apparent truth. It was as if I had never heard the doorman's words. For another month, I kept up my daily walks, kept looking at the building as we passed. By this time the doorman had become something of an acquaintance, always saying hello to Sophie and me as we passed.

One morning toward the end of the month, I was again passing the building when the doorman ran out to stop me. He handed me a piece of paper with a phone number on it and told me to call immediately. I did, and the next week I moved into the building. You see, one of the apartment owners suddenly had to move back to Europe to care for a sick relative. It turned out the man was from Cannes, my hometown, and that we shared more than a few acquaintances. His apartment was a beautiful, large studio, and Sophie and I lived there happily for many years. This simple story is the best example I can provide to illustrate the extraordinary power of intuitive knowledge, if only we are willing to access it. Intuition is always right—and we are wrong to ignore it.

Here then are three simple exercises that will help you begin to tune in and trust the hugely powerful faculty of intuition: (1) Journal writing, (2) Identifying the caller before you pick up the phone, and (3) Guessing what a person is thinking.

1. USE WRITING TO TAP IN TO YOUR INTUITIVE SYSTEM

This is so simple and so powerful. Unstructured "freewriting" provides a clear channel to the bottom of your intuitive knowledge pool. Forget spelling, grammar, penmanship, transitional sentences. All are completely irrelevant when freewriting—it must be free of all such considerations. It must also be handwritten—the arm and hand are, as you have probably already seen, the mind-body's natural conduits.

Start by clearing the contents of your mind—the 3Cs will help you here. Now pick up the pen and begin to write. Write at least a half a page of whatever emerges, whatever contents spill out of your mind-body onto the page. This emptying will help you tune in to your deeper stream. In time—perhaps after several sessions—your arm/hand/pen will begin to feel like a separate entity, working on its own to tap into and express the deeper contents of your psyche. Once your intellect shuts down, your subconscious finally gets a chance to speak, and boy, does it have a lot to say! The more you freewrite, the better your connection to your intuition, the more freely you will access your deeper truths. Be prepared for some revelations! Sooner rather than later, you will begin to experience some rather startling truths about yourself, your life, and other people in it. This is powerful, but it's also a little frightening—long-buried truths can be a challenge, can they not?

The benefits of freewriting go beyond making a reliable link to the intuition. Such writing changes lives entirely because of the power of the truths it catalyzes and brings to the surface. Be prepared for some changes, because once you start enjoying the many benefits of freewriting, you will never give up the practice. You will find yourself responding more deeply to people and events, for writing is above all a response to life, your response to your life. As a result, you will explore yourself and your spirit in ways you never imagined. For some, freewriting utterly renews the sense of self—some of my clients have told me that before they started this practice they were, in fact, complete strangers to themselves. Men, beware! Freewriting will put you in touch with your feelings! This might seem like a novel experience at first, but do understand the import of the "emotional information" you will be receiving. Give yourself time to process it. You may want to ask a good female friend to assist you here—I'm not kidding!

2. WHAT'S MY LINE?

This one is just plain fun. Next time the phone rings, guess who's calling before you answer. You'll be wrong more than you are right for a while, but then, especially on days when you are well balanced, your win-loss record will begin to improve. Once this happens, get ready to be astounded at how good you actually become at this. Eventually you will become simply uncanny. Once you have reached mastery here, you can impress friends with demonstrations of your incredible intuitive powers—don't worry, they'll suspect you of a setup!

3. MIND GAMES

This one is a lot of fun too. Begin with someone you know very well. At some point when you are together, but silent, imagine what the other is thinking. Then ask, and find out how you did. As with *What's My Line?* your initial results may be disappointing, but don't give up: they will inevitably improve. Soon people will begin to believe you are psychic. Guess what? You are!

The Mindful Warrior Walk

I hope it's not raining today, but even if it is, work on developing your mindful walking ability this morning. Remember, kiss the earth with your feet, touch the sky with your eyes. If you're getting good at this, add another dimension: develop awareness of the fresh air as it enters your nostrils (try to notice that it is cool when you breathe in, warm when you breathe out). More advanced yet, begin to develop awareness of your life force, your chi, coursing through your legs and arms as you walk. You'll arrive at your destination more refreshed than when you set out. *Fantastique!*

Day №6 Evening

Bonsoir! Did you tune in to your intuition today? We'll continue with that theme tonight. Here are your exercises:

1. Evening Cleansing Rituals

2. 3Cs Meditation Practice

3. Night Walk Meditation

Evening Cleansing Rituals

Need I say anything? Cleanse and enjoy the rest of your evening!

The 3Cs Meditation Practice

Calm, centered, and connected: that's the internal space you will need for the following meditation.

The Night Walk Meditation

TO DEVELOP INTUITION

Imagine a peaceful, moonlit summer night: commonplace, but always remarkable. You are calm. You are walking on a dirt road, deep in the country, moonlit fields on either side. A gentle breeze blows through your hair. The smell of flowers stirs your senses; the wind animates the fields, caressing the tall grass. The mating songs of cicadas fill the air. You are completely safe in the benign darkness of night.

Stop for a moment and look up to the starry sky. Let your mind seeks its furthest places. Transport yourself to deepest space. As you are enveloped in the night sky, let go of all concerns and desires. Set aside facts, release yourself from the grip of intellect. Open yourself up to the information from your deeper place. What are you aware of at this moment?

Walk farther down the road. What do you see? The objects you observe now may have metaphoric importance. What might they mean to you in your life? Are any symbols and patterns present along the way? Trust this information, but do not process or interpret it. Just observe.

Sense now the greater arc of your life's path. Intuit its meaning.

This is an excellent time to ask for guidance from some higher power, from some force that is both in you and beyond you. Be sensitive to all possible answers: verbal, visual, intuitive. Such answers may come now, or may come later as you begin to interpret this night's journey into the starry sky. Listen.

Think to yourself:

My intuition illuminates my path.
I am led toward my vision.
I am grateful for such guidance.

Know now that your intuition is always with you. It is always there awaiting your return. Return, return to the night sky.

Tip for the Evening
UNDERSTANDING SYNCHRONICITY

The wisest among us assure us that there are no accidents. What we so tentatively describe as *coincidence* is, in fact, just the visible tip of a much deeper reality, one most of us can only vaguely imagine. Our reality is more like a grossly incomplete picture drawn by a child with eyes half closed. We have all experienced the *uncanny*, but almost all of us come to disregard and eventually dismiss it. This is one of the unfortunate side effects of our rational orientation.

Take some time now to recall the *uncanny* at work in your life, the apparent coincidences sprinkled throughout our experience that we so easily dismiss. Compile a list now—you may wish to use a pen and paper. What are your stories of synchronicity? Recall them, then review and reinterpret them. What greater force was at work? How did such encounters serve to illuminate and identify your highest good and purpose? Make some connections; come to some conclusions about their meaning and guidance in your life. Bring your rational faculties to bear on these events. Try to uncover the elusive logic of the nonrational, of the apparent accident. Trust yourself to find the deeper significations of the language of synchronicity in your life. Tomorrow, be on the lookout for the subtlest of coincidences at work in your life. This is a rewarding faculty to develop—just as the vision of one shooting star leads to another, then another, then a hundred more. So too will your sightings of life's coincidences multiply until you will hardly believe that you once disbelieved!

Day №7   Morning

Congratulations. You have made it to the last day of Week Three of your Fresh Start! Give yourself the recognition you know you deserve. It's been a momentous week, hasn't it! Rejoice in it! Get ready for a day of joie de vivre! Here we go.

1. Morning Energizing Rituals
2. Three Ways to Experience Joie de Vivre

Morning Energizing Rituals

Enjoy these, today and every day.

Three Ways to Experience Joie de Vivre

Okay, as a reward for being so fantastic this week, I've prepared the best day of your life for you—are you ready!? So guess what, you are French today, French for the day! Run with me here, okay? You live in Paris, you speak impeccable French, and you count artists, poets, and high government ministers as your friends. Powerful executives seek your counsel. You give it freely, knowing that your higher nature should not be kept to yourself. Above all, you are known for your exquisite nature, your supreme faculty of *joie de vivre*. It is practically your trademark. To those who know you well, you seem to be the happiest person alive. Everything you do today, from the way you walk to what you eat, think, and say—all rise from your supremely French perspective. Are you ready? Let's begin!

1. THE FRENCH PHOTOGRAPHER

As you walk out today, remember that you are in Paris. Enjoy the beautiful city around you. "Feel good in your skin," as the French put it (*être bien dans sa peau*). Develop that French accent, you'll need it. Do you have a beret? All the better!

Okay, for your coffee break today, if you are a city dweller, find a nearby sidewalk café, preferably one that is at least nominally French. It should be on a corner, ideally should have checkered tablecloths and waiters in long aprons—you may have to use your imagination here! If you can't find a café, a park bench or other outdoor seat, ideally by a river, will do nicely. Make sure it has a pleasant view, in any case.

As you sit, enjoying your break, you will become a photographer, a very good, very French one, a fine art photographer who uses traditional film. With your keen *joie de vivre*–seeking eyes, you will observe everything around you: all the colors, the contrasts of light and shadow. Take all the time you need to develop these faculties. They are well within the reach of an ordinary American, I can assure you! And after all, you are far from ordinary! Once you have spotted a striking image, click your camera, capture this moment with your camera-like eyes. Is it two lovers kissing? Wonderful. An old lady with her lookalike dog? Click that shutter! Once you have taken your mental photograph, close your eyes and keep the scene fresh: make a lasting exposure.

Imagine next that you are back in your darkroom, developing your photos. See the image again as it begins to emerge out of the solution in your developing tray. Watch as it comes to life again on the vivid screen of the mind. Observe it hues and textures. Imagine now that you have stepped into the image. From within that world, you take in its many sights and sounds. Most importantly, as a part of the beautiful image, you can now experience absolute joy. Now, having opened yourself to the joyousness of the world you have entered, take the thumb and index finger of your nondominant hand and press them together to form a loop. Press moderately, firming up the loop, and say out loud three times: *Joie de vivre, joie de vivre, joie de vivre.*

Put an enormous smile on your face, take the deepest of breaths and fully absorb how good you really feel. Reopen your eyes now and smile at the world. You have your password to this world—it's *joie de vivre,* in case you haven't guessed. With these three magic words and the pressing together of your thumb and forefinger (the anchor), you gain access to such joy. The next time you crave or need escape, return to your French photographs. Here is always peace, tranquility, and joy.

Enjoy this wonderful therapeutic exercise today!

2. THE FRENCH GOURMET LUNCH

Today you are taking a good friend or loved one out for lunch. I mean it. Of course it will be French food (sorry, McDonald's fries won't cut it). You will order the Frenchest of foods possible. Frog's legs? Wonderful! They really can be superb. *Paté de fois gras?* Even better! If you are a vegetarian, no problem: try the *aubergines, asperges,* and the *ratatouille.*

Give serious consideration to a glass of Champagne or Beaujolais with your meal. Or, if you choose not to drink, you might prefer sparkling water, a Badoit, perhaps. Remember, today you are French—today you savor!

Since you are French, you will take your time considering the menu. You will call the maitre d' over so often he will become annoyed. This does not bother you in the least. Ask to speak to the chef about today's specials. (What does a waiter know but what he is told?) You inquire about all the ingredients of the dishes you are interested in, the method of preparation, the freshness of the fish, the regional origin of every item. If there is a sommelier (a wine specialist), solicit his advice before selecting your vintage. I hope you brought your credit card—being French is expensive!

When your food arrives, take some time before beginning to eat. Share a moment of appreciation with your companion. Wish him or her well and be sure to raise a glass in a toast before beginning: *sante!*

Savor every bite. Groan loudly when you get to a particularly flavorful item. If people stare, ignore them! Enjoy, my friend! *Bon appètit!*

3. THE FRENCH CONVERSATION

Here are the dos and don'ts: Do not, do not even consider, discussing business matters or any practical issues whatsoever. This is absolutely forbidden, okay? Instead, you will talk about your feelings in an absolutely heartfelt and honest way. Hold no true emotion back. Trust yourself here and encourage your companion to be equally frank ("frank" is just another word for French, be assured). If it pleases you, and if you are so inclined, philosophize to your heart's content. Make grandiose conclusions about the nature of man, the meaning of human existence. Speak of love, of course—young love, mature love, tragic love, the love that dares not speak its name: wax poetic about life's greatest gift. The most important rule of the game is to say only what makes you feel good to say. Let your heart and spirit soar, and enjoy the journey!

Day №7 Evening

Now wasn't that a day! I hope your photographs and your food and your conversation were divine, dear reader! *C'est la vie!* Know now that such days are not special days, but *every days*. You so deserve them! Please, promise yourself at least one of these days each month, will you now? Congratulations—great decision! Tonight's activities:

1. Evening Cleansing Rituals

2. 3Cs and Screening Room Practice

3. Victory Count

Evening Cleansing Rituals

All right, you know the routine!

The 3Cs and Screening Room Practice

With the joy of your magnificent day still resonating, you should have the best of all possible experiences with your 3Cs and in your Screening Room this evening. I'm sure you will find these practices richer tonight, probably the most vibrant yet.

Victory Count

You're at the conclusion of a momentous week! New experiences, new joys, new life. Surely you have many personal victories to celebrate. You have broken new ground, pushed the envelope of your spiritual life, challenged yourself and successfully met those challenges. You have initiated the most profound changes yet in your program of life change. By pushing your limits, you have made the momentous discovery that all limits are self-imposed; all limits are mere illusions. Your life has just begun, you've finally realized. You are becoming a beautiful, spiritual giant, your joy is *gargantuan*. Feed the giant of joy and enjoy his blessing in your life.

So ends the third week of your Fresh Start! I hope, dear reader, that you found the many immense joys that the rediscovery of the spirit can bring. You have sampled a wide range of reconnecting and re-awakening practices this week. I urge you to continue to use them next week, the week after, and the week after that. Use them for the rest of your life, why don't you! Know that these exercises are largely my own creations—yes, they work, of course they will always work, but once you get the spirit of *joie de vivre*, you will take your new life into your own hands, you will create and design your own methods for further awakening the spirit and the Promise within.

Thank you for taking this journey to the heart and soul of the human experience, dear reader. I hope and pray it has been a week of discovery and absolute joy. May you know nothing but joie de vivre in the months and days and years to come.

May you be supremely blessed!

May the lives of those you love be so blessed!

WEEK FOUR
DECLARING VICTORY

Victory

Victory

victory

VICTORY

VICTORY

Victory

VICTORY

A mind troubled by doubt cannot
focus on the course to victory.
ARTHUR GOLDEN,
Memoirs of a Geisha

The only victory that counts
is the one over yourself.
JESSE OWEN

Victory belongs to the most persevering.
NAPOLEON BONAPARTE

Expect victory and you
make victory.
PRESTON BRADLEY

7

The Practice of Changing the Rest of Your Life

There was once a man named George, a carpenter by trade. He was hardworking, slow to complain, honest in all his dealings. All his life he built houses, using skills handed down to him by his father. Though he wasn't paid well, and the man he worked for sold them for a handsome profit, his houses were his pride, models of traditional, enduring craftsmanship: sturdy and strong, plumb and square. Friends of his, other carpenters who knew the quality of his work and his scant reward, urged him to cut corners, to use lower-grade timbers—in short, to increase the profit of his labors by reducing their quality. Though he listened to their arguments patiently, he could not bring himself to build those kinds of houses.

One day, after many years of work, George made a life-changing decision. The next morning, he went to see this employer and told him he had had enough, he had worked hard all his life. Now he intended to spend his remaining days in the company of his wife and grandchildren. His employer argued with him, pressed him, urged him to continue his work, finally even offering to double his money. But George had made his decision. Still, the other persisted. Would he not build one last house before retiring? One last building before finally putting down his tools? Finally, though the decision irritated him greatly, he relented. Yes, he would build one last house.

The next week George began his work. Friends came by once again, urged him to work quickly, to use the cheaper materials available to him to get the work done as quickly and as cheaply as possible.

For the first time in his life, the advice landed on fertile soil. All his life he had built fine houses for others to enjoy—what would it matter if this final one didn't meet his usual high standards? And so he used poor lumber. He used materials that would need replacing after only a few years. He used fewer timbers, fewer nails. And he finished the house quickly, much faster than he had ever done before. Though it was a sad-looking thing, though he could take no pride in it whatsoever, it was done—he had at last completed his life's work.

The next day George went to his employer to give him the keys to the new house, shake hands, and say a final goodbye. The other came out to greet him, a smile on his face. The carpenter stood up, shook the man's hand, thanked him for the years of employment, and handed him the keys to the last house he would ever build. He turned and began to walk away, but the other stopped him. "George," he said, "I believe you're forgetting something." The man turned back, uncertain of the other's meaning.

"These keys belong to you, George. That house is yours. It's your home now, so enjoy it. I know you will—after all, you built it!"

· · · · · · · · · · · · · · ·

We come now to the final week of your Fresh Start program. Before I say anything at all, let me congratulate you, dear reader, for your strength, perseverance, hard work—above all, for your willingness to embrace lasting life change! Do not take the diligence you have shown these last three weeks lightly—such dedication is a remarkable thing. Please celebrate your victory now, for the fact is that there is no nobler human journey than the one you have begun—one whose purpose is new life and new direction. Let me salute you for your courage to change! Victory to you, dear reader!

Week Four is a week of maintenance, a week to solidify the many gains you have made these last weeks, a week to prepare for all the weeks to come, for the rest of your life's journey. The great news is that you have no new material or exercises to learn this week! You've got all you need now, dear friend—all the techniques and practices and meditations and visualizations to ensure that you go successfully forward to your Fresh Start Promise!

When you set out on your journey in Week One, I told you that you needed twenty-eight days to install the new conditioning required for lasting life change. You have accomplished this now—you have completed your installation, laid down the foundation that will serve you throughout your life. This week I will identify the essential Fresh Start practices that you will use every day from now forward to maintain your trajectory of life change. I will also provide for you a set of special purpose techniques to use as the need arises—for let's face it, there are still some challenging days ahead of you, days that will test you severely. Even though you have changed, the world has not! But you now possess all the tools and the techniques to overcome any future challenges. You now need only to understand how to put them into practice in your daily life. As you go forward into Week Four, remember the little story at the beginning of this chapter. Consider that during these past three weeks, you have been building the new house in which you will dwell. And you have maintained your highest standards. This house has the rooms you need to live a fully integrated, balanced, and joyous life. Please, then, do good work this week! This is not a house to be sold for profit, to be used by others, a vacation cottage to be used only a few months of the year. This is your house—this is where you will dwell!

You have taken the time, energy, and commitment to build it to the highest standards. You own it, and now you choose to maintain it! This week, begin the work that will keep it solid, reliable, enduring—inhabitable for the rest of your life! Shall we go forward now to learn the craft of house maintenance?

Checking In

As you now well know, your life has changed. The evidence is indisputable—there can be no question. No longer constantly harried by worries and fears, you now use your coping skills to disarm anxieties and create positive outcomes. Your neediness and confusion have lifted to reveal a clarified vision of what you truly desire, what aligns with your higher good, your higher life purpose. You have added new volumes to your subconscious library, you have engaged in the Language of the Heart to become more loving and supportive of yourself. You have planted the seeds of courage, strength, inspiration, passion, and joy in your inner garden. You have arrived at a greater calm and contentment within. You now feel good about yourself—know that this feeling is the result of the changes you have initiated. Your mind, body, and spirit are now working together in harmony. You have unity of purpose. You are more fully integrated. Your voice is more resonant and authoritative, because it is your breath and your power. You are more enthusiastic, you think more clearly, your thoughts are more focused. The 3Cs, the Screening Room, the meditations—all these are now working for you. You have greater energetic and emotional balance. This comes from your practice of *clearing* the negative, *creating* the positive—this grows from your chi-based body program. Finally, you experience far more joy, laughter, compassion, wonder, curiosity, and openness. Your deeper connection to the spirit is now at work!

So you have begun to reap the many rewards of such practices: wonderful! Truly wonderful! Now let us turn to your daily program to ensure that you will continue your journey to life victory. You have the necessary conditioning now, all you need to do is to maintain it, to carry it forward to greater successes, greater life changes—to make the shift you have experienced permanent. It's time now to move forward with courage and with the genuine expectation of new experiences, new life lessons, new life changes.

FRESH START MAINTENANCE PLAN: CLEAR, CREATE, CELEBRATE

Throughout our program, we've been keeping these key words in mind: clear and create. Now let's add one more. Whatever future problems you might face, whatever future doubts might arise, remember these three key words:

Clear, Create, Celebrate

This is what it all comes down to, dear reader: clear, create, and celebrate. In these three words you possess a pure distillation of the core Fresh Start program for life change.

First:

Clear the mental obstacles and hindrances, the anxieties, the agitations, the fears that stand in your way.

Then:

Create your vision of specifically targeted life change, create the body balance needed for your change, create the loving kindness and connection to the spirit required for change.

Finally:

Celebrate your accomplishments, your successes, your victories, your joys, and your *joie de vivre!*

Fresh Start now becomes a three-step program—you see we have added *celebrate* to *clear* and *create* (to celebrate the completion of your foundational work!). Each step is important, each step leads to the next, each depends on the one before—together, these three steps make an integrated program of lasting life change. Here, then, is your daily practice. For today, for tomorrow, for the rest of the week, and for the rest of your life.

- Daily practice of your 3Cs meditation (in the morning or in the evening, while you walk, while you wait, while you work). This meditation is indispensable. It is foundational. It is the *clear* that begins the process and upon which all things depend.

- Daily practice of the Screening Room to visualize and manifest the specific, concrete life changes you have chosen for yourself, to maintain the life changes you have already set in motion. This is *create!*

- Daily use of the Language of the Heart to support you in your life change, to cultivate loving kindness and compassion for the self. This is also *create.*

- Daily practice of chi-based body rituals to renew, rejuvenate, and sustain your life force, to give you positive, vibrant energy, to activate and aid both the *clear* and the *create* processes.

- Daily practice of the chapter 6 "Awakening the Spirit" techniques to maintain humor, openness, curiosity, compassion, honesty, connection to self and others. This, too, is *create.*

- Daily Victory Count to acknowledge your progress and your success, to maintain gratitude for yourself and to the universe for allowing you such life success. This is *celebrate.*

If you are concerned about the time required for these daily practices, remember that you have successfully done them for three weeks now—you have found the time, found the energy, and, as a result, experienced their many benefits. Know that you will become more efficient in their use, and their benefits are lifelong. Trust that you will find the time and you will, dear reader, you will! Your life will have its ups and downs (though much less dramatic ones); it will have good days and challenging days. On your good days, these exercises and techniques will serve as an enhancement, an amplification of your joy. On your challenging days, they will be your medicine, providing the tools to meet those challenges. They will keep you going, they will keep you on your path, they will keep you strong and make you stronger still.

FRESH START DAILY SCHEDULE

Here now is your Fresh Start cookbook: One recipe for the good days, one for the challenging days.

. . . .

FRESH START RECIPE FOR A GOOD DAY

. . . .

Daily Program

Morning

1. Morning Energizing Rituals (Chi Belly Massage, Morning Breathing Practice, Chi Body Massage)
2. Mindful Eating Practice
3. Warrior Walk and Declaration
4. Practice Joie de Vivre
5. 3Cs during the day

Evening

6. Evening Cleansing Rituals (Wrist Shake, Arm Swing, Spinal Cord Breathing)
7. 3Cs and Screening Room
8. Victory Count

Description of a Good Day

You feel happy upon waking. You had peaceful dreams. You feel energized, completely refreshed. You are happy for the new day, happy to be you. Good things have been happening lately: the day before, and the day before that, all week, in fact! Life has been pretty good, actually. Last night you counted your victories and it took you longer than ever—there are a lot to count these days!

While Still in Bed

Conduct your morning energizing rituals (Chi Belly Massage, Chi Body Massage, Morning Breathing Practice). If you slept in, or if you are in a rush, do fewer repetitions: five instead of nine.

The morning rituals are the best possible way to begin the day. They have made a fundamental difference in the lives of all who use them. When *you* use them, you will re-establish your energetic connection to your body, you will maintain your acute chi awareness, you will be able to balance your emotional and energetic systems. You will dramatically reduce the amount of stress in your life. As result, you will strengthen your immune system; suffer fewer colds and illnesses. Chi energy is an absolute key to maintaining a healthy body and mind.

At Breakfast

Eat slowly (as time allows), maintain mindfulness of the many tastes and textures of your food and drink. Doing so will help you maintain your optimal healthy weight.

Heading Out the Door

Just before you leave your home, take a few minutes for your Warrior Walk to prepare you for a successful day. Use your Victory Within declaration: *I Can. I Do. I Will.*

During the Day

Whatever you do, keep the smile of contentment on your face, find and engage in little joys and humorous moments—these will ensure your *joie de vivre*. Practice kindness, compassion, acknowledgment. Attract and be drawn to those who are honest, those with integrity. Connect to them. Share your life with them. Practice your 3Cs whenever you get the chance—at your desk, while waiting for the elevator, whether standing or sitting—to realign mind, body, and spirit.

In the Evening

When you come home, do your cleansing rituals immediately (Wrist Shake, Arm Swing, Spinal Cord Breathing). If you are pressed for time, do three rounds of each, rather than the full nine. Sit down to do your 3Cs to prepare for your visit to the Screening Room, which will reinforce your vision of change. Before going to bed, count your victories; hug yourself by wrapping your hands around your shoulders in a self-embrace. Voilà! Victory to you!

. . . .

"VICTORY WITHIN" RECIPE
FOR A CHALLENGING DAY

. . . .

Daily Program

Morning

1. Breath Therapy for Emotional Release
2. Chi Belly Massage
3. Chi Body Massage
4. 3Cs and Screening Room
5. Warrior's Armor (Armor of Light and Sword of Fearlessness)
6. Declaration: I can. I do. I will.
7. Use the Language of the Heart
8. Compassion and Humor Engagement

Evening

9. Evening Cleansing Rituals (Wrist Shake, Arm Swing, Spinal Cord Breathing)
10. Emergency Release Therapy
11. Sound and Finger Therapy
12. The 3Cs and Screening Room
13. Your Choice of Meditation

Description of a Challenging Day

You woke up feeling tired. You have stress, anxiety. Perhaps you've received some challenging news recently, had some upsets at work or in your relationships. Your energy is sluggish. If you've been experiencing anger lately, you want to cry (if you are a woman), or you feel more emotional than usual (if you are a man). You'd like to cover your head with the pillow and stay in bed all day, but of course you can't, you've got to go to work.

To Begin the Morning

Practice the Breath Therapy for Emotional Release, exhaling deeply through the mouth to expel negative energies. Then treat yourself to a tender Chi Belly Massage, paying close attention to your power center at the navel. Sit on the edge of the bed and give yourself an extra long, extra loving Chi Body Massage.

Practice your 3Cs meditation. Then, move to your Screening Room practice. Use a healing visualization: picture yourself the way you would like to be and feel: healthy, calm, centered, free of stress and anxiety.

Use your anchor, make a fist, and declare three times (increasing the volume each time): *Victory is mine. Victory is mine. Victory is mine.*

Heading Out the Door

Before leaving your home, suit up in your armor of light—for the extra protection you need today—and bring your sword of fearlessness too. Imagine yourself as a powerful warrior as you step out the door and into your day. Wear your armor all day, sword at the ready. And use your affirming incantation: I can. I do. I will.

During Your Day

Focus all attention and all energies inward—don't give them away today. Save compassion for others for another day: today, all compassion is yours! Be absolutely kind and loving toward yourself. Find humor in every situation possible. Focus on being kind and loving towards yourself. Treat yourself with deep compassion. Avoid people who drain your energy; surround yourself with people who radiate energy (grab some for yourself—you can repay the debt another day!). When you get a moment, use your Sound Therapy: practice the first four healing sounds (lung sound for anxiety, kidney sound for fear, liver sound for anger, heart sound for sadness).

In the Evening

As soon as you get in the door, practice the evening cleansing rituals. Focus your attention on eliminating all your stresses and anxieties. Shake your wrists and release whatever is no longer serving you. Do your Arm Swings, abandoning all control to the movement of your limbs.

Finish the evening rituals off with the Spinal Cord Breathing. Now use the Emergency Release Therapy. Pick up this book and see pages 140–142 if you need to review. If you are still not feeling as good as you'd like, repeat this technique two more times. Practice your Sound and Finger Therapy, 3Cs, and Screening Room. Use one or more of the meditations—especially the Rowboat to release your burden of worries, and the Diamond of the Heart to develop loving kindness for yourself. Know that life will get better—it will!

· · · · · · · · · · · · · · · ·

There you have it, dear reader—all the techniques you will ever need in your practice of life change. Use them, practice them, engage yourself fully in them. These are the techniques that will maintain your life's house, keep it in the best possible condition. They will serve you throughout the days to come: they and they alone are the key to your Fresh Start Promise!

LOOKING FORWARD

As you continue along your path of change, know that you will come to develop absolute faith in your new abilities. You will develop an appreciation for the wisdom of your life choices. You will be empowered; you will take full responsibility for life itself. Instead of blaming others for your problems when things go wrong, blaming your fate on bad luck or your own inadequacies, you will accept that you still have some more work to do; you will take up this work in earnest.

You will no longer be passive, you will no longer be caught up in waiting and hoping for better things to happen. You will, instead, make things happen, bring about the changes you desire. You will now fully understand that you are in control of your destiny and the conditions of your life. You will be liberated by the knowledge that you have absolute freedom of choice, that you are no longer bound by older, limiting patterns of behavior, by the excessive controlling forces of others. Above all, you will feel empowered, in charge, knowing that you are a positive, actualizing force in your own life. The challenges that come your way will no longer frighten you—instead they will excite you because you know that they provide the opportunity for greater life victories. You will have a bountiful supply of courage, knowing in the depths of your heart that you can transform negative situations to achieve positive outcomes. You will have acquired a new conditioning.

You will surprise yourself by thinking and acting in productive ways. You will be more relaxed. Victories will come frequently, so often that you will one day conclude that you are the victor of your own life! Let this Daily Guide become second nature.

Daily Guide for Your Fresh Start Promise

- Start the day with a smile on your face to welcome new opportunities.
- Put on your Armor of Light for protection against negativity, and carry the Sword of Fearlessness for courage and strength.
- Walk with confidence, your lungs filled with air, your head touching the sky and your feet kissing the earth.
- Remember to stay calm, centered, and feel connected to the power of universal energy.
- Welcome every challenge as an opportunity to test your courage and develop your strength of character.
- Stay focused on what you desire to change, not on what has happened in the past, which cannot be changed.
- Ask yourself what you are learning from this situation, instead of why this situation has happened to you.
- Change your attitude and behavior in order to achieve different results.
- Look for a clear intention before you decide to take any action.
- Do not wait for a miracle; create one.
- Do not search for perfection; accept being human.
- Affirm and repeat every day: I can, I do, I will!

FINAL THOUGHTS

So, dear reader, go forward now with your week. Follow your daily schedule of core practices and reinforce your spirit-based practices and meditations. To review them, see the Index of Practices and Meditations at the beginning of the book.

This is the week you bring it all home! Use the regular recipe and daily program schedule on good days; use the special-purpose recipe and schedule on challenging days. Know that with the Fresh Start program you cannot fail, you can only move forward to greater life change. You are a novice no longer. Today you are a graduate. Let me now salute you as a fully trained and equipped warrior of the Fresh Start Promise! I will leave you with one last story to ready you for your fourth week, the many weeks yet to come.

In final preparation for their lives as Buddhist monks, the Dalai Lama leads his novices into a special room for a crucial initiation ceremony. In this room, the novices are told, will be manifested all their human fears, doubts, and anxieties. Their purpose is to walk through this great room to the single door on the other side, a door that is the passage beyond all fears, doubts, and anxieties. They must enter the room, face their fears, confront their doubts, and wrestle their demons. Success is to reach the door, keeping the feet moving and the mind steady. Success depends, thus, upon absolute clarity of purpose, undistracted focus on the door leading to the light.

This rite of passage is powerful, for with it, such monks fully confirm for themselves that they have moved above and beyond the human mind's delusions of the human mind—the illusions that condemn them to a life of suffering.

As you pass through the final week of your Fresh Start, keep this story foremost in your mind, for it applies to you as well. Life is full of distractions and apparent obstacles that pull us away from our goals, that mire us in the fantasies and delusions of the mind.

The solution isn't a secret. It isn't hidden. It is, in fact, within plain sight. Success depends only upon moving forward with absolute awareness of your vision for change. Do not let other people, or other forces, pull you away from it. Remind yourself daily of your life's new purpose. You have a new identity now; you are more than capable of overcoming life's challenges, doubts, and distractions. With such concentrated awareness, you will pass through every obstacle that arises on your path; you will walk through the door to new life victories, a novice no longer.

And now I would like you to give some serious consideration to your future! Yes, you have done a remarkable job these last three weeks. The changes you have set in motion are truly momentous. But I must ask you one final but crucial question: What will you do now? Will you finish off the week, put the book away, be grateful for your four weeks of enhanced balance and joy, then return to your life as you once lived it? If you do, I obviously can't stop you (since I don't know where you live—otherwise I'd pay you a visit!).

I urge you not to abandon your program of life change! Continue your Fresh Start, dear friend! Do not give up all that you have gained! Do you intend to make your changes permanent, to realize future growth? If this is your intention—and nothing in this world would make me happier—do something right now, before you put down this book and walk away. Commit yourself to lifelong change! Are you ready? I hope so, dear reader, I truly hope so!

So yes, one last time, pick up that pen! You have it? Wonderful! You will now sign one final contract with yourself, one that you must consider legally binding! You may be tempted to treat this lightly: "Yeah, yeah, I'll sign the thing and be done with it." Think again. This contract with yourself is lifelong—and irrevocable. This contract, once signed, will send an unequivocal message to your *self,* to your mind-body-spirit, to the universe. It commits you to lifelong change, to a life filled with compassion, wonder, honesty, and *joie de vivre.* Make this commitment now, my friend. Make it because with that commitment, everything will change.

Okay, are you ready? Wonderful! Here, then, is your contract. Sign on the dotted line and be forever grateful for your loving commitment to yourself and your program of lifelong change. Congratulations, dear reader! Go forward now in your practice of change, forward to joy, and forward to *joie de vivre!*

THE VICTORY WITHIN
LIFELONG VICTORY CONTRACT

Once again and forevermore, I _____, recognize that:

> » I am a unique individual, with a special purpose.
> » I am meant to have a rich and fulfilling life.
> » I am worthy of respect and self-respect.
> » I have within myself gifts, talents, strengths, and unrealized potential.
> » I create unconditional love and acceptance for myself.
> » I can choose a kind and caring attitude toward others.
> » I am capable of making my dreams a reality.

Therefore, I commit to:

> » Using my daily practices on my journey to greater life growth and change.
> » Continue my practice of being kind and loving toward myself and others.
> » Continuing to look within for spiritual intelligence and guidance.
> » Continue to view every challenge as an opportunity to further my dream.
> » Continuing to discard outdated, counterproductive, and anxiety-producing ways of thinking.
> » Continuing to use the 3Cs and the Screening Room to further advance my life change.
> » Continuing to use my body-based practices to clear negative energies and emotions, to create positive energies and emotions.
> » Continuing to use my healthful eating practices so that I may experience peace, balance, and contentment.
> » Continuing to amplify my connection to the spirit so that I may experience compassion, understanding, intuition, joy, and *joie de vivre*
> » Forging ahead to greater life victories, greater life change.
> » Continuing to trust and believe that my life has purpose and significance

I will pursue my goals with clear intention and honesty. I am willing to continue to do the work required to transform my attitude and my life. Nothing and no one can stop me from manifesting my vision of the person I desire to be.

_____   _____
Signature   Date

Suggested Reading

THE MIND

Bandler, Richard, and John Grinder. *Frogs into Princes: Neurolinguistic Programming.* Boulder, CO: Real People Press, 1979.

Bien, Thomas. *Mindful Recovery.* New York: Wiley, 2002.

Corcoran, Barbara. *Use What You've Got and Other Business Lessons I Learned from My Mom.* New York: Penguin, 2003.

Eker, T. Harv. *The Secrets of the Millionaire Mind.* New York: Harper-Collins, 2005.

Fisher, Stanley. *Discovering the Power of Self-Hypnosis.* New York: Newmarket Press, 2002.

Grinder, John, and Richard Bandler. *The Structure of Magic.* Palo Alto, CA: Science and Behavior Books, 1975.

Hanh, Thich Nhat. *The Miracle of Mindfulness.* Boston: Beacon Press, 1999.

Henderson, Charles E. *Self-Hypnosis for the Life You Want.* Biocentrix Publishing, 2003.

Kabat-Zinn, Jon. *Wherever You Go, There You Are.* New York: Hyperion, 1995.

Umlas, Judith W. *The Power of Acknowledgment.* New York: IIL Publishing, 2006.

The Body

Burmeister, Alice. *The Touch of Healing.* New York: Bantam, 1997.

Chia, Mantak, and Mancewan Chia. *Sounds That Heal.* 2006.

Guiliano, Mireille. *French Women Don't Get Fat.* New York: Knopf, 2004.

Jaffe, Marjorie Jaffe.*The Muscle Memory Method.* National Book Network, 1997.

Kliment, Felicia Drury. *The Acid Alkaline Balance Diet.* New York: McGraw-Hill Professional, 2002.

Lewis, Dennis. *The Tao of Natural Breathing.* Berkeley, CA: Rodmell Press, 1996.

Sinett, Todd. *The Truth About Back Pain.* New York: Putnam Penguin, 2008.

Virtue, Doreen. *Chakra Clearing.* Carlsbad, CA: Hay House, 1998.

Wu, Baolin, and Jessica Eckstein. *Qi Gong for Total Wellness.* New York: St. Martin's Press, 2006.

Young, Robert O., and Shelly Redford Young. *The pH Miracle.* New York: Warner, 2002.

THE SPIRIT

Byrne, Rhonda. *The Secret.* Hillsboro, OR: Beyond Words Publishing, 2007.

Dalai Lama and Howard C. Cutler. *The Art of Happiness.* New York: Penguin/Riverhead, 1988.

Dyer, Wayne W. *The Power of Intention.* Carlsbad, CA: Hay House, 2005.

Gee, Judee. *Intuition: Awakening Your Inner Guide.* York Beach, ME: Weiser Books, 1999.

Roth, Gabriella. *Sweat Your Prayers: Movement as Spiritual Practice.* New York: Penguin Putnam, 1998.

About Edwige Gilbert

For over twenty years, Edwige Gilbert has been a leader in the field of wellness and well-being. The focus of her groundbreaking therapeutic work has been to adapt holistic, Eastern, metaphysical, physical and fitness-based modalities to the fields of health and stress/energy management. Her clients range from Lehman Brothers, to Citibank, to Verizon, to St. Luke's Roosevelt Hospital, New York. As a presenter, practitioner, facilitator, and motivational speaker, Edwige has appeared throughout the United States and abroad.

Edwige's work has been featured in such magazines as *American Health, Allure, Women's Fitness,* and the *Avenue.* She is the creator of Nouvelle Yoga, the Zen Workout, and the Fresh Start Program. Edwige holds a degree from the American College of Sports Medicine, a BA in counseling psychology, and multiple disciplinary and interdisciplinary certifications in clinical hypnosis, neuro-linguistic programming, Qi Gong, Yoga, Sivananda Yoga, substance abuse counseling, and hypnotherapy.

Edwige presents and teaches at prominent hospitals, industry centers, health clubs, corporations, substance abuse centers, and wellness events throughout the United States. She has worked intensively with leading international and national medical professionals, and her clients include celebrities and leaders in both business and media.

A native of Cannes, France, Edwige has dedicated her life to helping others through the practice and therapy of mind-body awareness. Situating herself at the confluence of Eastern and Western perspectives, Edwige has helped hundreds of clients discover their own personal pathways to intentional harmony, energetic balancing, and peak potentiality. Her approach to wellness and well-being is based on the balanced integration of mind, body, and spirit in the pursuit of sustained personal growth and lasting life change.

Fresh Start represents a summation of nearly thirty years of professional work in the field of human wellness. An integrated, interdisciplinary program dedicated to helping others achieve specifically targeted and sustainable life change, the Fresh Start Program brings together a profoundly successful blend of therapeutic techniques and practices from around the world: a wide range of psychological, body-based, and spiritual disciplines. In philosophical terms, Fresh Start represents a shift from the unstable and unpredictable domain of the external, to the essential and integral domain of the internal.

Edwige currently presents, teaches, and conducts the Fresh Start Program in New York City, in West Palm Beach, Florida, and throughout the country. She conducts Fresh Start workshops seminars and retreats around the country and around the world. For further information and/or registration in the Fresh Start Program, or to book Edwige for a seminar, consultation, or public speaking engagement, please visit the New Life Directions website at www.newlifedirections.com.

Sail into Your Dreams
8 Steps to Living a More Purposeful Life

KAREN MEHRINGER

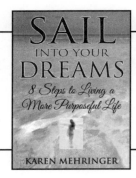

Sail into Your Dreams is the perfect book for anyone who's ever asked, "Is this all there is to life?"

Unsatisfied with her busy life in Seattle, Karen Mehringer embarked on a six-month, life-changing ocean odyssey to Australia, Indonesia, Fiji, and, most importantly, toward the joyful, fulfilling life she had always wanted.

You don't have to leave land to make your dreams come true. Karen shares the wisdom and practical tools she learned on her ocean odyssey, showing us how to focus on what truly matters. Journal entries and inspiring stories from Karen and others highlight how to slow down, nurture yourself, connect with others, and tap into your life force energy—the source of infinite possibilities.

This eight-step program will help you assess your life and eliminate toxic relationships, emotional trauma, physical clutter, and debt—making space for new experiences that awaken your passion and spirit.

978-0-7387-1053-2
5 x 7, 240 pp. $13.95

To order, call 1-877-NEW-WRLD
Prices subject to change without notice

The Power of Time
Understanding the Cycles of Your Life's Path
PAULINE EDWARD

Don't wait around for life to "happen." Develop a solid, successful life plan with guidance from numerologist and life coach Pauline Edward.

Whether your goals are personal or professional, *The Power of Time* can help you take advantage of the natural cycles influencing your life. Is this a time of new beginnings or are you ready to reap the rewards of your efforts? Simple calculations based on numerology (derived from a birth date) will reveal where you are in each nine-year cycle and what to expect from each year, month, and day. Once your life path is mapped out, it's easy to pinpoint the best times to start a new job, focus on family, launch a business, take time to reflect, make a major purchase, complete a project, expand your horizons, and more.

Also included are worksheets and exercises—practical resources to help you clarify your life purpose, set goals, identify potential obstacles, and map out your future with confidence.

978-0-7387-1149-2
7½ x 9⅛, 240 pp. $15.95

Get Out of Your Way

*Unlocking the Power of Your Mind
to Get What You Want*

Layton Park

Beliefs, dreams, fears, goals—they all begin in the mind. Hypnosis offers a way to tap into the subconscious mind to produce amazing life changes.

From professional sports to the business world, hypnosis has helped millions achieve their desires. In *Get Out of Your Way*, Layton Park explains how and why hypnosis works, and shares "universal laws of mind" for transforming our belief system to allow our dreams to come true. Readers will learn how to clarify goals, construct effective affirmations, and engage these affirmations for positive life-changing results. Also featured are compelling case histories—true stories from the author—demonstrating the success of self-hypnosis.

Included with the book is an audio CD of easy-to-follow self-hypnosis techniques that can be used for accomplishing career goals, losing weight, quitting smoking, resolving phobias, and fulfilling a wide variety of personal ambitions.

978-0-7387-1052-5
6 x 9, 240 pp. $21.95

To order, call 1-877-NEW-WRLD
Prices subject to change without notice

How to Get Everything You
Ever Wanted

ADRIAN CALABRESE, PH.D.

When Adrian Calabrese's faithful car bit the dust, she was broke and had already maxed out seven credit cards. She went looking for her dream car anyway, and by the end of the day she was the proud owner of a shiny Jeep Cherokee. It was all because she had found the secret formula for getting what she wanted. Not long after that, money began flowing in her direction, and she paid off all her debts and her life turned around. Now she shares her powerful method of applying ancient concepts of inner wisdom to everyday life. Starting today, anyone can begin immediately to get everything out of life he or she desires.

978-1-56718-119-7
7½ x 9⅛, 264 pp. $15.95

Spanish edition:
Obtenga éxito
978-0-7387-0215-5 $14.95

The Secret of Letting Go

Guy Finley

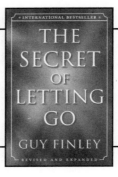

Llewellyn is proud to present the revised and expanded edition of our best-selling self-help book, *The Secret of Letting Go* by Guy Finley. Featuring an attractive new cover and fresh material, this Finley classic has been updated inside and out.

With more than 200,000 copies sold, Guy Finley's message of self-liberation has touched people around the world. Discover how to extinguish self-defeating thoughts and habits that undermine true happiness. Exploring relationships, depression, and stress, his inspiring words can help you let go of debilitating anxiety, unnecessary anger, paralyzing guilt, and painful heartache. True stories, revealing dialogues, and thought-provoking questions will guide you toward the endless source of inner strength and emotional freedom that resides within us all.

978-0-7387-1198-0
5³⁄₁₆ x 8, 312 pp. $14.95

The Secret Wisdom of a Woman's Body
Freeing Yourself to Live Passionately and Age Fearlessly
PAT SAMPLES

Pat Samples counters America's fixation on youth with a revolutionary approach to midlife and aging. She teaches women how to listen to their bodies—incredible archives of our life experiences—and draw upon the emotional and spiritual wisdom within.

This life-changing odyssey begins with developing new awareness and appreciation for your changing body—the precious home for the spirit. Once you trust the body as a teacher, you can learn from childhood experiences, past traumas, heroic moments, and other personal stories recorded there. True accounts from the author illustrate how she and other women found healing and relief from grief, stress, anger, addiction, and other painful issues. Featuring practical exercises and fun activities, this remarkable guide to body wisdom will also inspire self-exploration, spark creativity, rejuvenate your spirit, and ease the fear of aging.

978-0-7387-1159-1
6 x 9, 264 pp. $15.95

Unlocking the Healing Code
Discover the 7 Keys to
Unlimited Healing Power

DR. BRUCE FORCIEA

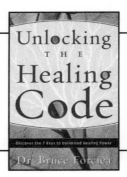

Have you wondered why traditional medicine as well as herbs, homeopathy, and other alternative practices all work? They are all linked by a universal, mysterious field of energy that is alive with useful information. This healing information flows from the source to us across four channels, and anyone can learn how to activate these channels to heal injuries and recover from illness.

Bridging the gap between traditional and alternative healthcare, Dr. Bruce Forciea introduces seven keys to unlocking this unlimited healing power. His techniques, useful for both patients and practitioners, help you choose and apply complementary healing methodologies—such as creative visualization, vitamins, herbs, magnets, microcurrents, light, and chiropractics. True stories, including the author's own experience with recovering from chronic illness, highlight how numerous people have found relief using this groundbreaking program for healing.

978-0-7387-1077-8
6 x 9, 216 pp. $14.95